THE ANCIENT WORLD

A Reading and Writing Approach

Ralph Sawyer
Peter Townsend

National Textbook Company
a division of *NTC Publishing Group* • Lincolnwood, Illinois USA

Acknowledgments

The authors and publishers would like to thank the following copyright holders for permission to include material in this book: The British Museum, pp. 28, 46, 124; The Israel Museum Jerusalem, p. 60.

Illustrated by Peter Townsend

Contents

Chapter One   The Stone Age: *Humans Begin*   2

Chapter Two   Egypt: *Land of the Nile*   24

Chapter Three   Israel: *The Promised Land*   58

Chapter Four   Greece: *Land of Heroes*   78

Chapter Five   Rome: *A Great Empire*   106

Chapter Six   China: *Land of History*   136

Chapter Seven   The Middle Ages: *Into Darkness*   166

Epilogue   *The End of the Story*   192

Glossary   194

Index   199

Chapter One

The Stone Age

Humans Begin

The Division of Time

The age we live in today is often called the **Nuclear Age**. This age or period dates from 1945 when the first atomic bomb was exploded. Humans like to divide time into periods. Years, months, days, hours, minutes, and seconds are all divisions of time.

A human life can be divided into six ages:

- infancy
- childhood
- adolescence

- young adulthood
- middle age
- old age

During each of these ages, people usually carry out activities that are typical of their stage of life. For example, during childhood people learn to read and depend on parents. In old age, people usually retire from their jobs and slow down in physical abilities and activities.

◤ The Ages of History

The same approach is used for the history of the human race. We attempt to divide time into sections so that we can better understand the whole picture. Each period of human history has been dominated

Activity
Your first activity is to name the six ages of people today. Draw a table like this:

The Ages of Human Life		
Age	Years	Activities
1. Infant	0–2	Eat, sleep, cry, learn to walk, talk
2.		
3.		
4.		
5.		
6.		

Complete the columns of the different ages. What you have done is divided or *classified* people. You have also described each *classification*.

This is a natural urge of human beings—to "put things in boxes" or describe things in sections. That is the way we learn to understand ideas—by breaking them down into subsections.

Write and Discuss
Which of these theories seems the most likely to you? Give reasons for your answer.

by an event or an invention. Some of these events still have an impact. For instance, the ability to use iron was a great advance. We still have the benefit of iron and steel for thousands of everyday uses.

There is **geological** evidence (from the study of rocks) that the earth has been here for many millions of years. It is still not accurately known when animal life first appeared on earth.

There are many different theories about the beginning of life on earth. Here are three that are popular in Western society. One belief is that the world was created by God in six days as described in the Book of Genesis in the Bible. This is believed to have happened about 6,000 years ago.

Another theory states that the world was created by God but not strictly in six days as described in the Bible. According to this theory, God started life on earth and since then life has evolved and refined into the various plant and animal forms that we see today. Humans became the creatures chosen by God to rule the earth.

The third theory is that a star exploded and spun off gases and particles that came together as a separate new planet. This new planet was first a molten hot globe that gradually began to cool. At first the conditions were too hot and hostile for any possible life, but eventually a primitive form of single-celled animals began to appear in the sea. From this primitive form of life began a long process of evolution. This theory is sometimes called the **Evolution Theory**.

Back in Time—The Ages of Peoples

Nuclear Age	Started with explosion of atomic bomb	AD 1945–Present
Motor Age	The use of automobiles for business and pleasure	1910–1945
Electrical Machine Age	The use of electricity in factories, transportation, and lighting	1870–1910
Steam Age	The use of steam engines in factories, farms, and railways	1810–1870
Age of Empires	When Europe controlled overseas colonies in Africa and Asia	1700–1870
Age of Cities or Urban Age	The growth of cities because of factories	1810–1900
Age of Kings and Queens	When Europe and most of the world were ruled by single rulers	1300–1800
Middle Ages	The age of knights, castles, and crusades	1100–1400
Dark Ages	The age of defensive forts, raiders, and feudal lords	500–1100
Roman Age	Roman armies and law controlled most of Europe	100 BC–AD 500
Age of Ancient Civilizations	The civilizations of Greece, Egypt, Israel, and China	2000 BC–AD 100
Iron Age	The Hittites of what is now eastern Turkey were the first to make iron weapons and tools	1200 BC–AD 100
Bronze Age	Mixing copper with tin, Middle Eastern peoples made semi-hard tools and weapons	2000–1200 BC
Copper Age	Soft copper ornaments, tools, and weapons were used over a wide area of Middle East and China	3000–2000 BC
Stone Age	Early settlements of people using primitive stone axes and tools	750,000–3000 BC

Write and Discuss

"The Ages of Peoples" table classifies the history of humans into sections, or ages. Discuss with your classmates what each of these ages means. Why do some of the ages overlap in time? Why do the dates for the Stone Age have question marks?

Write and Discuss

Here is a collage of the Story of Humans. Each picture represents a feature of one of the Ages of Peoples.

1. Can you identify each of the six Ages in this picture?

2. Name each Age.

3. Write the six Ages in chronological (time) order.

4. Write one feature of each of these Ages.

■ *The Ages of Peoples
through time.*

Write and Discuss

1. Most of the earth's crust has cooled down. Where are there still active volcanoes in the world today?

2. Can you name any of these volcanic mountains?

The Evidence of Evolution

There is strong evidence that the world was once a very hot place. All over the world there are layers of rock and whole mountain ranges that obviously were once molten rock. The center of the earth is still very hot, and from this center gush lava, steam, and boiling mud through the volcanoes and steam geysers that have broken the earth's crust. The cooling process is still obviously in action.

Another piece of evidence is the skeletons of animals that became extinct thousands of years ago. Humans have left no record of these animals, and so it is reasonable to suggest that the animals lived on earth long before humans appeared.

The most well known of these are the dinosaurs. Complete skeletons have been dug up in the United States and near the salt lakes of South Australia.

Dating even farther back than the complete skeletons of dinosaurs are the **fossils** of earlier animals. Fossils are the remains of ancient plants or animals. Over thousands of years the skeleton of the plant or animal has been covered by mud or soil. This has slowly turned to rock, trapping the skeleton within. Sometimes the skeleton has completely rotted away, leaving only the imprint of its shape in the rock. The illustrations show an example of a plant fossil and an animal fossil.

Write and Discuss

1. Some dinosaurs were **carnivorous**, others were **herbivorous**, and some were **omnivorous** in their eating habits. What does each of these terms mean?

2. What were the main enemies of dinosaurs?

3. Why are so many fossil remains found in the La Brea tar pits in California?

4. What kinds of fossils have you seen in geology museums?

■ *The imprint of a fossil fern found on a slab of coal in an Australian mine. This fossil was found 300 meters (about 980 feet) below the surface.*

■ *The fossil of an ancient flying reptile. This fossil was found set in limestone at the bottom of a deep lake in Switzerland.*

Write and Discuss

1. What conditions on earth would be favorable for the existence of living creatures?

2. Why was it easier for creatures to live in the sea rather than on land?

3. Approximately when would the dinosaurs have appeared on earth?

4. Why do you think it was so long before humans appeared on earth?

The Time Clock of the World

If the earth's total existence was spread over a 12-hour clock face, this is what it would look like:

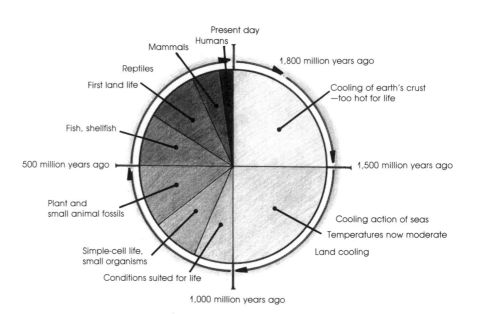

The Beginning of Humans on Earth

Skulls and bones found in central Africa show that people have lived on earth for well over one million years. Only a few of these bones have been found, so we do not know exactly what these early people looked like.

The shapes of the skulls seem to show that these early people looked slightly different from us but were still real people, not apes or half monkeys. It is important to note that the human species does not have a direct fossil or skeleton link with monkeys or apes. However, the shape of the skull, the small brain cavity, and the shape of the skeleton suggest that there has been some evolution in the formation of humans since they first walked the earth.

The development of humans is shown by the chart. The artist's impressions are made from the different types of skulls that have been found in such places as Africa, China, and Europe. The most recent type of skull that has been found is **Homo sapiens** ("thinking man" or "wise human being"). This human closely resembled us in physical appearance.

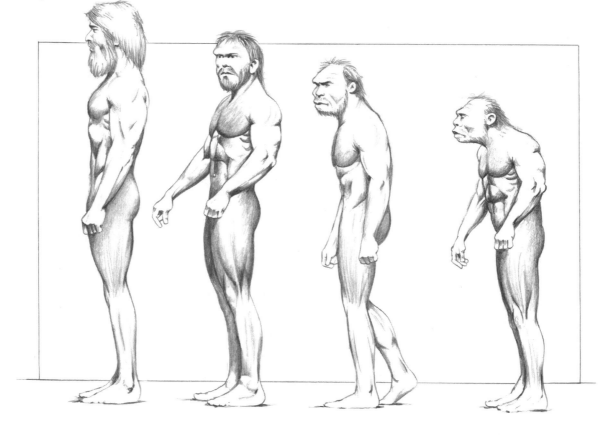

■ *Modern Homo sapiens.*   ■ *Neanderthal (early Homo sapiens).*   ■ *Homo erectus.*   ■ *Homo habilis.*

Ancient Humans				
Name	**Time on earth (approximate)**	**Appearance**	**Tools and relics found with bones**	**Possible customs and way of life**
Modern Homo sapiens—"thinking person" or "wise human being"	20,000–3000 BC	Like modern people.	Stone sickles or grass cutters. Stone axes, spears, arrows, brick and stone houses.	At first hunters and food gatherers. Later these Stone Age people became farmers and animal herders.
Neanderthal humans (early Homo sapiens)	375,000–40,000 BC	Smaller than modern people. Skulls with thick bone forehead and large teeth. Strongly muscled.	Hand axes, animal skin scrapers, stone borers. Bones of mammoths and Ice Age creatures.	Hunters of animals and food gatherers. Lived in warm caves. Used fires. Drew animal cave paintings. Buried their dead.
Homo erectus—"upright person"	1 million–375,000 years ago	Short (approx. 1.4m or 4'7" tall); small forehead; small brain. Powerful neck and jaws.	Early hand axes. Used fire to cook animals.	Primitive hunters. Fire was their main tool for life.
Homo habilis—"handy person" or "skillful human being"	2 million–1 million years ago	Not enough bones to tell exactly.	Very basic chipped stone tools. Crushed and cracked animal bones found with human bones.	Did not use fire. Basic food gatherers and hunters.

Write and Discuss

1. Can you identify which group of ancient humans these people belong to?

2. What skills have they got that earlier humans did not have?

3. What clues are there about this family's way of life?

4. Would this family be a part of a larger tribe or would it live on its own?

5. What sorts of things are these humans doing that separate them from the rest of the animal world? For example, they are using hand tools.

6. How are these people using their environment to stay alive in this icy countryside?

 # Establishing Dates

On the chart there are estimates of the age of the various types of humans that have been discovered. How do scientists come to these estimates?

First, anthropologists carefully study the area where the bones are discovered. Usually the bones are found deep in the earth with layers of ash, silt, rock, or soil above them. From this it is possible to make a rough estimate of the number of years it would have taken to cover up the remains.

Scientists today use Geiger counters and computers to measure the radioactivity of bones. The amount of radioactivity gives an estimate of the age of the bones. The method is known as **carbon dating**. Another more up-to-date method is known as **argon potassium dating**.

■ *An Ice Age family living in a cave.*

The Coming of Homo Sapiens

Some of the ancient skulls dug up are very similar to our skulls today. These skulls are often discovered with improved stone tools and with signs of well-built houses and villages. These people are called *Homo sapiens*, meaning "thinking person." This name indicates that these people were most like us today in intelligence.

Archaeologists have been able to date Homo sapiens back to about 375,000 BC. They are able to do this by linking their knowledge with that of geologists.

■ *A cave skull.*   ■ *Homo sapiens skull.*

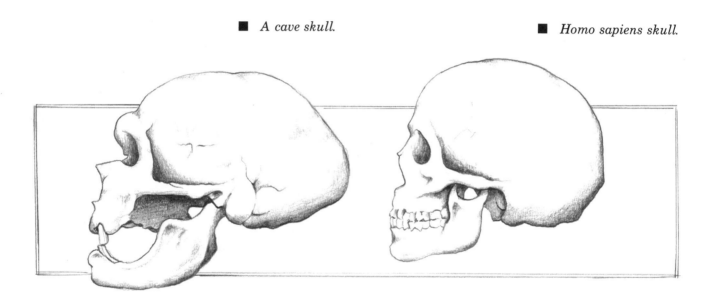

Activity

This is a drawing of a skull that was found buried in a cave. Compare the cave skull with that of a later Homo sapiens. Can you write down three main differences in head structure?

Geologists have dated rocks and glaciers to show that there were several Ice Ages, when the ice from the Poles crept across the earth toward the equator. During these cold times the level of the rivers and the oceans was low. The ocean and river levels rose again when the last Ice Age melted and caused the flooding of harbors and river valleys.

During the height of the last Ice Age, the Northern Hemisphere looked like this.

There is rock and fossil evidence that there were several Ice Ages. These were times when the world cooled and the ice packs of the North and South Poles extended toward the equator. At the present time the world is gradually becoming warmer, and the ice caps of the Poles are melting. This means that the oceans are rising. Geologists and scientists estimate that as the earth warms up over the next thousand years, the ice caps of the Poles will melt even further. The sea levels of the world could rise up to 100 meters or 328 feet above their present

■ *Area covered in ice.*

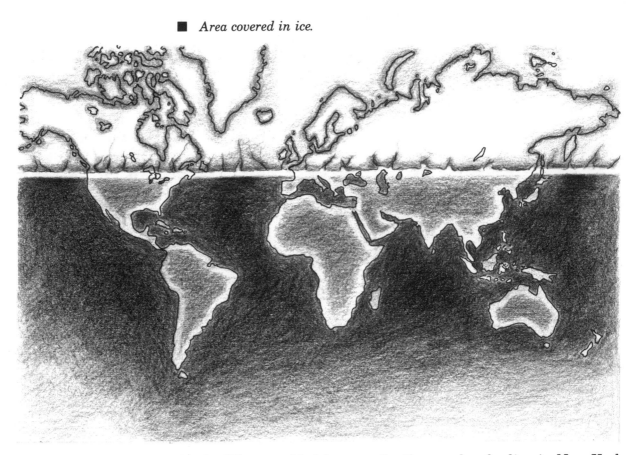

levels. What would this mean for the people who live in New York City? It is possible that archaeologists one thousand years from now will find old cities below the surface of the sea!

Skulls and skeletons have been found in southern Europe and China that date back to before the last Ice Age. The diagram shows how Homo sapiens was dated back to at least 20,000 years ago. The examples of Homo sapiens found in Britain and Germany were found as the diagram shows.

Geologists have been able to establish that the gravel and rocks found above the tools and bones were the result of a glacial river during the last Ice Age of 20,000 years ago. This means that these remains of Homo sapiens date back to at least the height of the last great Ice Age.

■ *Possible sea level 2990 AD.*

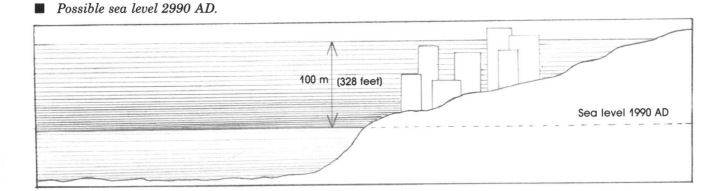

100 m (328 feet)

Sea level 1990 AD

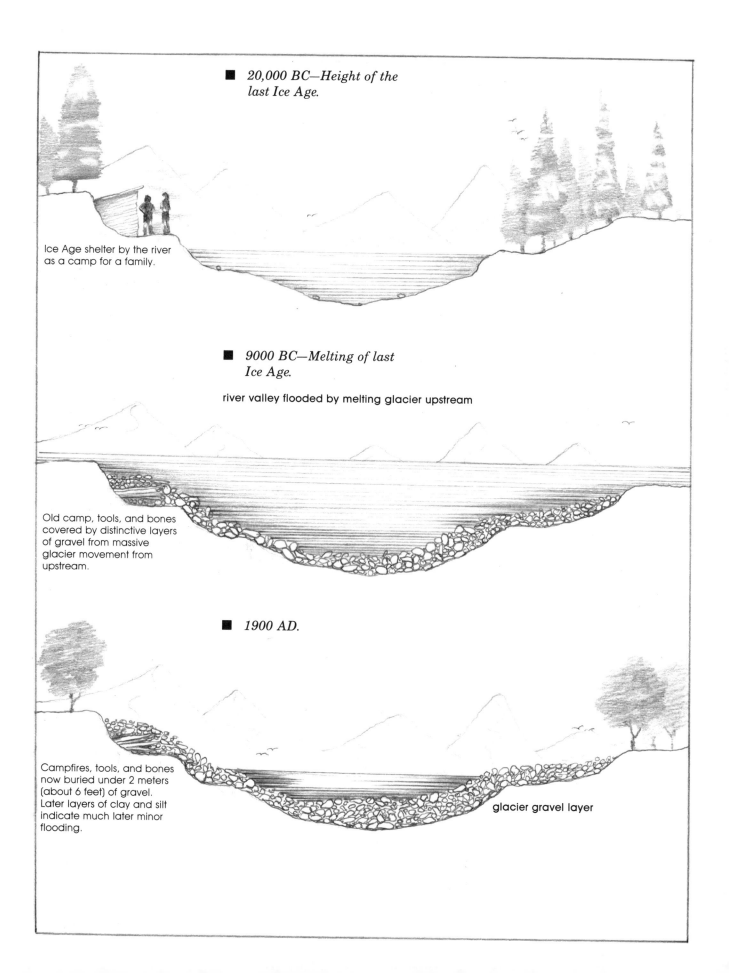

■ *20,000 BC—Height of the last Ice Age.*

Ice Age shelter by the river as a camp for a family.

■ *9000 BC—Melting of last Ice Age.*

river valley flooded by melting glacier upstream

Old camp, tools, and bones covered by distinctive layers of gravel from massive glacier movement from upstream.

■ *1900 AD.*

Campfires, tools, and bones now buried under 2 meters (about 6 feet) of gravel. Later layers of clay and silt indicate much later minor flooding.

glacier gravel layer

The Old Stone Age People—Our Direct Ancestors

The evidence of bones and skulls shows us that Homo sapiens did not look very different from modern people. There was great progress in the way Homo sapiens lived during the next era. The remains of tools, houses, burial sites, and cave paintings show us that people changed rapidly in the way they lived.

The first Homo sapiens who have left evidence of settlement are called **Paleolithic** or *Old Stone Age people.* By 10,000 BC, these Old Stone Age people were spread across a wide area from Europe to China and America.

What Were Our Ancestors Like in 10,000 BC?

To begin with, the Old Stone Age people had adapted well to their environment. They were emerging from the last terrible Ice Age and only the fittest and most adaptable humans had survived. The Old Stone Age people survived by living in small family groups rather than in large tribes. This was necessary if they were to get enough food to eat. The earth was too cold to grow food, and wild berries and fruits were not plentiful in the cold areas.

The best hunting group was about 5 adults with a total family group of approximately 25. If they killed a pig or a deer, they would have enough to feed the whole group for nearly a week. The scraping tools that have been found were used to scrape the animal skins clean so that the skins could be used for clothes and warmth.

The early Stone Age people did not try to tame the land by cultivating, clearing brush, or building towns. They fitted in with the harsh environment. When food became scarce, the family groups split up or moved to new hunting areas.

We have evidence that the Old Stone Age people were more technologically advanced than earlier humans. Their tools included bone needles, fishhooks, arrowheads, and harpoon spearheads.

These people were able to learn new methods and ways of making tools. They probably traded with other clans or tribes in such items as salt and weapons. They must have believed in an afterlife, because they buried their dead in ceremonial graves. The paintings found in the caves show that Old Stone Age humans used their memory and their imagination. Some of the symbols and signs indicate a belief in magic or the supernatural.

■ *Hardy survivors of the last Ice Age struggle to stay alive.*

Activities

1. Make a list of the skills and customs of the Aborigines and Eskimos that link them with the Old Stone Age people. You might begin with the table of skills and customs in this book.

2. Discover what factors forced the Aborigines and Eskimos to leave their Old Stone Age ways and come into the modern world.

Survivors from the Old Stone Age

Humans advanced from the Old Stone Age or Paleolithic Age to more modern people. They were able to do this because of climate changes and their ability to learn new ways from other groups. In our recent human history, there have been several survivors of the Old Stone Age who have not changed very much.

Two examples of these are the North American Eskimos and the Australian Aborigines. Until the mid-nineteenth century, these people still lived in the Stone Age. They did not change because the harsh climates they lived in supported their traditional ways of life as wandering hunters and food gatherers. Their isolation from other large groups and lack of trading meant that they did not learn and adopt new ways.

The New Stone Age People

In the study of ancient peoples, there are two types of experts. **Archaeologists** are people who dig up buried cities, skeletons, and relics from the past. Archaeologists scientifically study these relics in order to discover how old they are, who made them, and how they were made.

Archaeologists are expert detectives. From only a few discovered items they have been able to reveal a lot about Stone Age people.

Anthropologists use the discoveries of archaeologists to describe how different people lived. Anthropologists describe how people earned their living and what they believed. They study the links between the different peoples of the world and are sometimes able to discover common features.

For example, most early human settlements have been found near rivers. Buried in the mud near these rivers, archaeologists have discovered signs of a more technologically advanced Stone Age people. They have found mud bricks, stone walls, stone bowls, and clay pottery. Most important, stone and bone sickles have been found. These were used for cutting grass or grain crops.

Anthropologists have called the people of this new stage of development **Neolithic**, which is Greek for "New Stone Age People." This New Stone Age period is roughly between 7000 BC and 3000 BC. After 3000 BC the use of cooper, bronze, and iron began, and the Stone Age began to be replaced by a new stage of civilization.

The map of Europe and the Middle East shows the places where these New Stone Age settlements have been discovered near rivers. As well as these places, early Neolithic settlements have been found in Thailand, China, India, and Central America.

Nineteenth-Century Survivors of the Old Stone Age—Skills and Customs		
	Aborigines	Eskimos
1. Land and climate	Harsh dry climate. Not many natural fruits.	
2. Size of communities		
3. Main occupations		Hunting seals. Fishing.
4. Weapons		Bone harpoons, spears, and fishhooks.
5. Houses		
6. Food and how they obtained it	Kangaroos killed by spears. Seeds and roots gathered.	
7. Clothing		
8. Artwork and religious customs		

Write and Discuss

1. What are the names of the rivers on the map where early settlements were found?

2. In what modern countries are these rivers?

3. Two regions where ancient settlements were found were Mesopotamia and Egypt. Identify these two areas on the map.

4. Which areas on the map would have a:
(a) Cold climate? What would the village people do for food in these areas?
(b) Mild or temperate climate? What would they grow in these areas?
(c) Hot, dry climate (with the river to help them)? What would they do to grow food in these parts?

5. As well as growing food, these New Stone Age people had herds of tame animals for food. What sort of animals would they keep for food? Why was it easier for these river people to keep animals than it was for the Old Stone Age people?

■ *Early Neolithic settlements in Europe and the Middle East regions.*

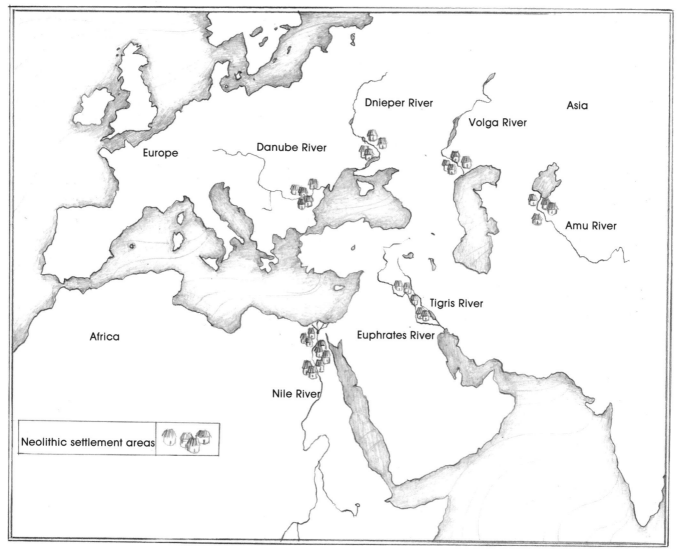

Dnieper River

Volga River

Asia

Danube River

Europe

Amu River

Tigris River

Euphrates River

Africa

Nile River

Neolithic settlement areas

The Growth of Material Civilization

If you measure the level of civilization by material development (what objects people have), the Neolithic people of Sumer, Babylon, and Egypt made great progress after 3000 BC. Now that people lived in one place and grew their food, they had a definite advantage over previous people.

The grain that they grew and the animals they kept meant they could store food. This meant each family did not have to hunt or gather food *every* day as in the Old Stone Age.

Write and Discuss

The five inventions were important in ending the simple Stone Age way of life and in beginning new, large-scale civilizations in Mesopotamia and Egypt from 2000 BC onward. How did simple farmers form large communities like Sumer, Babylon, or Egypt? Discuss in particular how each of the five inventions could have changed the simple farming way of life to a much more advanced way of life.

Activity

Write a paragraph with the heading "Out of the Stone Age." Write about the things you see in the picture. How do you know these people are out of the Stone Age? How is life easier for them? Do they have to grow everything for themselves?

People could spend time building houses of sun-dried bricks or stone blocks. They could make simple furniture and begin to weave cloth from wool. Clay pots and heavy grinding stones made food preparation easier. Clay pots were used to boil meat and grain for the first time.

Now that people lived in villages, a simple form of government or leadership was necessary to keep basic rules on such matters as ownership of land.

An occasional surplus of grain made it possible to trade grain for salt, for dried fish from the coast, or, later, for gold coins. In some places along the rivers, large villages grew into trading centers that became the future cities of places like Babylon.

About 3000 BC, a series of inventions or developments greatly speeded up the changes in the people's way of life:

1. The wooden plow pulled by a tame ox

2. The use of the wheel for irrigation and wagons

3. Writing, which first developed at Sumer. Clay slabs were used to write on for trade and government.

4. The use of sails and wind as sources of power for boats along the rivers

5. The use of copper and, later, bronze to make cooking utensils and weapons of war

■ *A market town in Babylonia, around 1500 BC. The Stone Age is finished for these people.*

The End of the Simple Stone Age Life

Look at the artist's impression of a market in a village on the Euphrates River in Babylonia about 1500 BC. Look at the details of the picture carefully. There are obvious signs that the primitive Stone Age is finished and material progress has been made.

New Stone Age People of the Twentieth Century

One of the last peoples of the world to leave the New Stone Age were the people of Papua New Guinea, north of Australia. As late as 1966, New Stone Age tribes were discovered in the Western Highlands of the island of New Guinea.

The New Guinea people are roughly divided into two main groups—the coastal people and the highlands people. The coastal people live along the coast or on rivers. They came into contact with white people in the 1870s.

The people of the highlands were not discovered until the 1930s. These Stone Age people were discovered after the invention of the camera, and so we are lucky to have photos of them at work and play. Because they lived in tropical regions, they may not have lived exactly like the people of Egypt or Europe.

■ *A New Guinean first sees Europeans on a visiting trading ship in 1875.*

■ *Gold miner Mick Leahy meets a Stone Age New Guinea Highlander for the first time in 1930.*

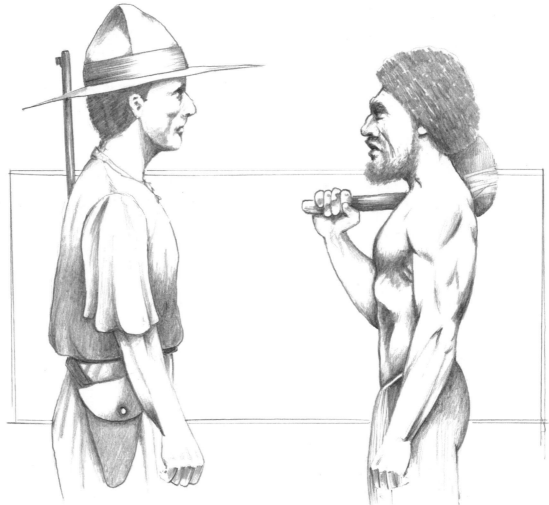

How Did the Stone Age People of New Guinea Live?

The Stone Age people of New Guinea were mainly gardeners and growers of food. They used a **slash-and-burn** system before they planted their gardens. The illustration shows a slash-and-burn garden site like those found in New Guinea.

Some Stone Age New Guineans lived in sago (a kind of palm) swamps along the river. These river people lived in small groups.

Write and Discuss

1. Why didn't the New Guineans completely clear the land?

2. How would burning off the garden site help the garden?

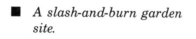

A *slash-and-burn garden site.*

River people of Purari River in south-central Papua New Guinea.

Write and Discuss

1. Why did the river people live in houses on tall posts?

2. How did they travel up and down the river?

Other Stone Age New Guineans were mountain people who lived in small round houses on the ground. The walls of these houses were woven together from palm leaves. These people were hunters rather than food growers. They were much smaller than the average New Guinean native.

The primitive highland people had many ceremonies for big occasions, such as funerals or weddings. The whole clan met together, sang songs, had a feast, and danced for days. This was called a *sing-sing* in their language. As well as singing, these people would have mock fights between the clans. Sometimes they forgot they were pretending and began a real fight.

As part of the ceremonies, the mountain people might wear bird of paradise feathers headdresses. One of these headdresses might have 10 birds' feathers in it and could be worth five pigs—a very high price.

■ *Chuave highlander.*

Write and Discuss

The people of Papua New Guinea have mostly left the Stone Age now and live a more modern life. What sorts of things have been introduced into their lives from modern people that would have greatly changed the native people's lives? For instance, how would a steel axe or a radio have changed their lives? What other modern inventions would be very useful to these people?

Write and Discuss

1. What did the New Guinean highlanders use for music with their dances?

2. What types of weapons did these people use in their fighting?

■ *New Guinea highlanders during a sing-sing at Mount Hagen, 1960.*

Chapter Two

Egypt

Land of the Nile

The Growth of River Civilizations

At the same time that communities were growing at Sumer and Babylon, other river valleys of the world were developing separate civilizations. In China, India, and Egypt, Stone Age farmers were developing large-scale communities.

- Why did early civilizations grow up along major rivers?

- What part did the river play in developing civilizations?

- Why didn't the river communities remain small villages rather than join together as a nation?

- Did each river community grow different crops or was there one type of crop that was common to all of them?

Written records do not go far enough back to completely answer these questions. Instead, historians have made up a series of **hypotheses** or theories about the beginnings of these civilizations. Look at the following hypotheses and decide which ones seem to give reasonable answers to the questions above.

Write and Discuss

1. Which of these hypotheses answer some of the questions above?

2. Can you think of any other reasons why people might have combined in river communities, for example, defense?

3. Are there any river communities in the United States today? Are these areas densely populated? What occupations do the people have in these areas?

4. Imagine that you are an archaeologist working in the Indus Valley (in what is now Pakistan). Report on the discovery of an invention that explains why the people were able to establish a thriving river community, for example, a metal sickle or a picture of an efficient plow.

---

1. The annual flooding of the river provided a layer of silt, which enriched the soil and made it suitable for farming. This rich land was able to support large numbers of people in a small area. Even in dry periods the river valley would be attractive to people because of the availability of water for irrigation.

2. The growing of wheat and barley was possible because of the reliable water supply. These grains could be stored for use by towns or villages on the riverbank. This left leisure time for other activities, such as building houses.

3. The surplus food supply meant that people could specialize in jobs, such as building, copper smithing, or trading. In this way, stable villages and towns grew up around these markets and craft centers. It was no longer necessary for everyone to be involved in hunting or farming.

4. Annual flooding and irrigation require large-scale cooperation and direction. From this need, larger communities developed. These groups created leaders and a form of government. The pharaohs of Egypt probably began as such leaders.

5. Settlements along rivers were more likely to be open to new ideas and techniques from other communities farther along the river. The river was a highway for the spread of new ideas.

6. A chance invention or discovery could have dramatically increased food production, thus making larger settlements possible. Such an invention could have been an irrigation wheel or a grinding stone to crush seed into flour.

The Land of the Nile

The Nile Valley produced one of those ancient civilizations. The country of Egypt has been in existence for about 5,000 years. Even today, most of the people still live along the river valley of the Nile. The capital of Egypt is now Cairo. The main crops of Egypt are cotton, rice, and sugar. Most Egyptians are still peasant farmers working on small farms in the river valley.

The River Nile has always been the center of Egyptians' lives. The river has three sources. The White Nile runs between the Sudd, a swamp in southern Sudan, and Khartoum. The Blue Nile and the Atbara River begin in the mountains of Ethiopia. Each year when the snows melt, the river floods.

Between July and October this flood reaches the lower parts of Egypt. The Ancient Egyptians called this the *flood season*. The months between October and March were known as the *growing season*. During this season, the farmers busily planted their gardens. The hot sun and the damp, rich soil combined to produce plentiful crops. Between April and June was the dry season. As the river dropped, the farmers

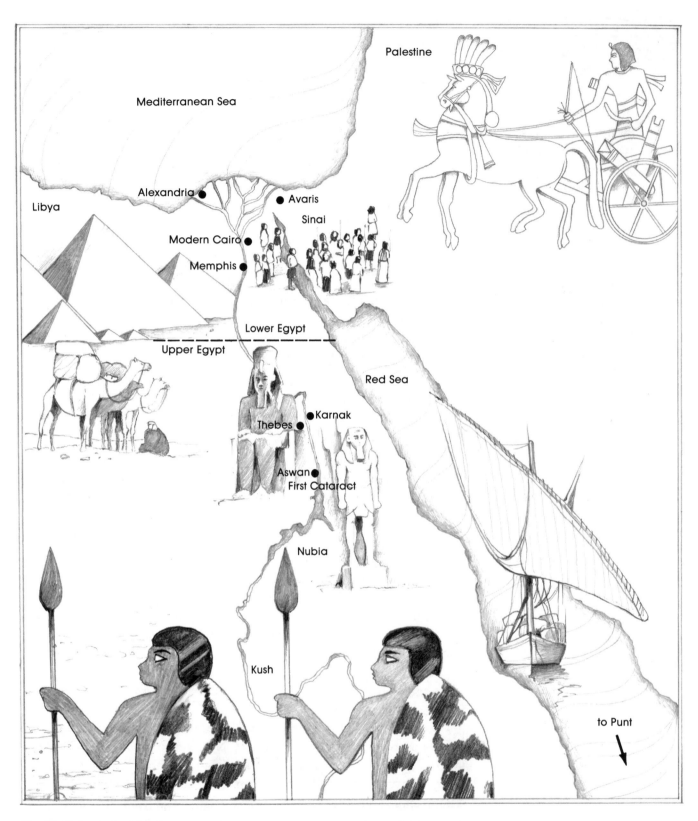

■ *Life along the Nile in*
Ancient Egypt.

Activity

Draw these three diagrams in your notebook. Label your drawings with the names of the three seasons of the Nile River. Write in the months for each of these seasons.

Write and Discuss

What advantage was there in having a large stone on one end of the shadoof?

■ *Irrigating during the dry season with a shadoof.*

■ *The Nile Valley during the three seasons of the year.*

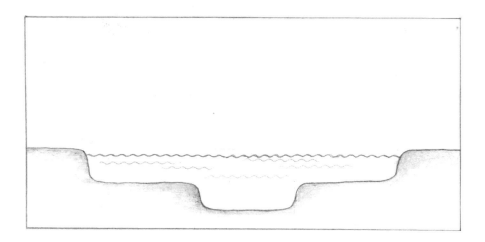

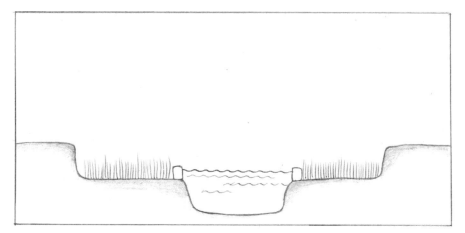

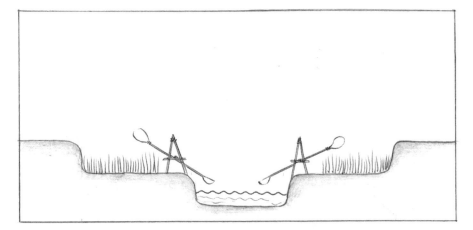

used irrigation until the river dropped below the irrigation wall level. Then they used a simple form of water transfer called the **shadoof**.

In modern Egypt the farmer has two growing seasons in one year. A huge dam at Aswan controls the annual flooding to prevent the damage of an uncontrolled high flood. In the dry season, water is released from the Aswan Dam to maintain the river level at irrigation level.

Growing Grain in the Nile Valley

The growing of grain (wheat and barley) required the efforts of many people. One person could grow some wheat, but for feeding large numbers the type of farming required a team of workers and a large farm with oxen plows and a wheat silo or granary. Look carefully at the Egyptian wall picture.

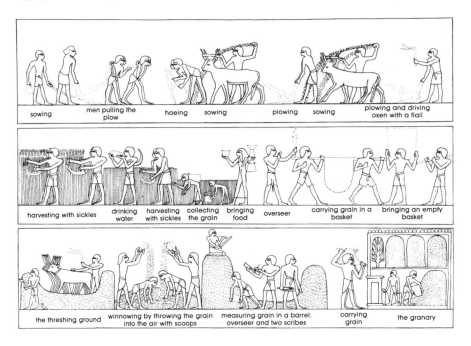

■ *The steps in wheat farming. (Courtesy of the British Museum.)*

The Pharoahs of Egypt

In the earliest days of Ancient Egypt, there were two distinct kingdoms along the Nile River. Lower Egypt was near the mouth of the river in the delta region. Upper Egypt was the settlement along the riverbank farther up the river.

In about 3100 BC, King Menes united both kingdoms. He became known as the first pharaoh to rule the whole of Egypt. He created a new capital at Memphis, which was at the border of Upper and Lower

■ *King Menes kills an enemy in his battle to unite Egypt under his rule as the first pharaoh.*

Egypt. King Menes began what was known as the first **dynasty**, or line of pharaohs. Altogether, there were thirty-one dynasties, or families of pharaohs. They ruled Egypt from 3100 BC to 332 BC.

This is a remarkable achievement. For almost 3,000 years pharaohs ruled Egypt. The longest modern line of kings is the family dynasties of English kings that go back 900 years. The dynasties of Egyptian kings lasted 2,000 years more than this.

The complete story of all these dynasties is much too large for this book. A summary of the dynasties is set out below.

Early Dynasties (3100–2686 BC)

Important pharaoh: Menes
Important events:

■ The two kingdoms are united by Menes.

■ Memphis is made the new capital city.

■ The idea of pharaoh as a divine person is established.

■ Egypt's boundary is extended to Nubia, a country south of the First Cataract.

The Old Kingdom (2686–2181 BC)

Important pharaohs: Djoser, Khufu
Important events:

■ Djoser builds the Step Pyramid.

■ The religion of afterlife and the elaborate burial of the dead become a feature of the life of Egyptian pharaohs.

■ Egyptian expeditions go to Palestine and East Africa to obtain raw materials of ebony, timber, ivory, and gold.

■ Pharaoh Khufu builds the Great Pyramid of Giza. His son builds the Great Sphinx, which has the body of a lion and the head of a pharaoh.

■ *An Egyptian trading ship.*

First Intermediate Period
(2181–1991 BC)

Important pharaohs: No strong pharaohs at this time.
Important events:

■ Central government in Memphis begins to fall apart. Many of the tombs and pyramids are robbed and destroyed. Records say that the "lower classes have become our masters."

■ Feudal princes set up **nomes** or small states along the river. The **nomarchs** of these states pay little attention to the pharaoh.

■ Thebes begins to be the most important city up the river rather than Memphis.

The Middle Kingdom
(1991–1786 BC)

Important pharaohs: Mentuhotep II, Amenemhet III
Important events:

■ Egypt was united again under the strong Pharaoh Mentuhotep II. Thebes becomes the new capital for 50 years.

■ The temple for the hidden god Amon was built at Karnak near Thebes.

■ Trading expeditions were sent to Crete and Punt in eastern Africa. Military expeditions were also sent to Lebanon and Syria.

Second Intermediate Period (1786–1554 BC)

Important pharaohs: Hyksos kings, Kamose
Important events:

- Invaders from Asia take over Lower Egypt. This new dynasty of Hyksos kings introduces horses and chariots to Egypt.

- The Hyksos also introduce iron weapons, which are far superior to the copper weapons of the Egyptians.

- The Theban pharaoh Kamose eventually defeats the Hyksos and drives them out of their capital, Avaris, and back into Palestine.

- *Horses and chariots became important in Egypt after they were introduced by the invading Hyksos kings.*

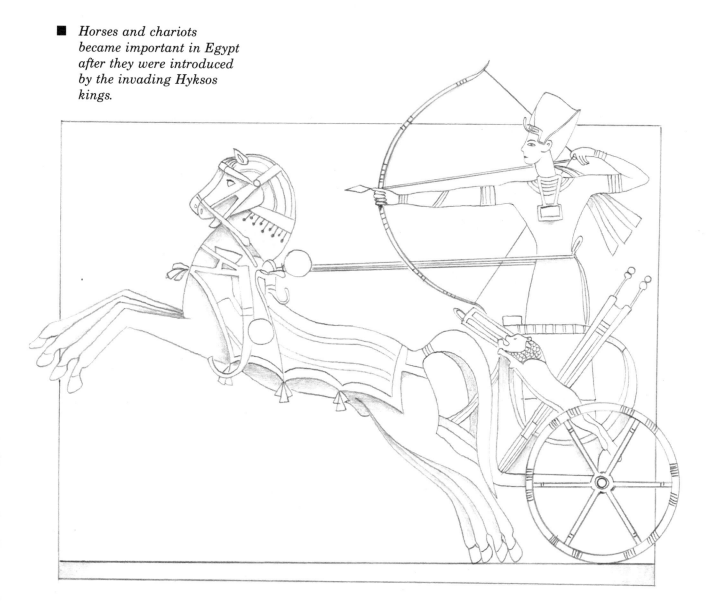

32

The New Kingdom (1554–1070 BC)

Important pharaohs: Queen Hatshepsut, Akhenaton, Thutmose III, Tutankhamen

Important events:

- Egypt enters a 500-year period of greatness. Egypt now has a great army.

- Under Thutmose III, Egyptian power is spread to Babylon.

- The Hebrew people are captured and spend 80 years as a captive people in Egypt.

- Akhenaton abolishes all gods except Aton, the sun god.

- Tutankhamen, the young pharaoh, is buried with all his equipment for later life. His tomb is the only tomb to be found untouched in modern times.

- Queen Hatshepsut becomes a powerful pharaoh.

- *Later pharoahs, such as Tutankhamen, were buried in tunnels in cliffs, rather than in pyramids.*

- *Pharoah Akhenaton worshipping Aton, the sun god.*

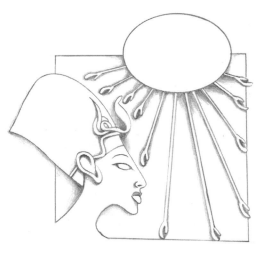

Third Intermediate Period (1070–656 BC)

Important pharaohs: Sheshonk, Piankhi
Important events:

■ The powerful pharaohs of the New Kingdom are now replaced by foreign pharaohs from Libya and Nubia. These foreign pharaohs adopt Egyptian ways and customs.

■ The robbing of tombs becomes a national pastime. Even pharaohs use the wealth of the tombs to finance their own rule. Some attempts are made to shift the buried pharaohs and their wealth to new secret tombs.

■ Piankhi, an Ethiopian prince from Kush, establishes many of the old art forms and restores buildings; his dynasty is cut short by the Assyrian invasion of Egypt.

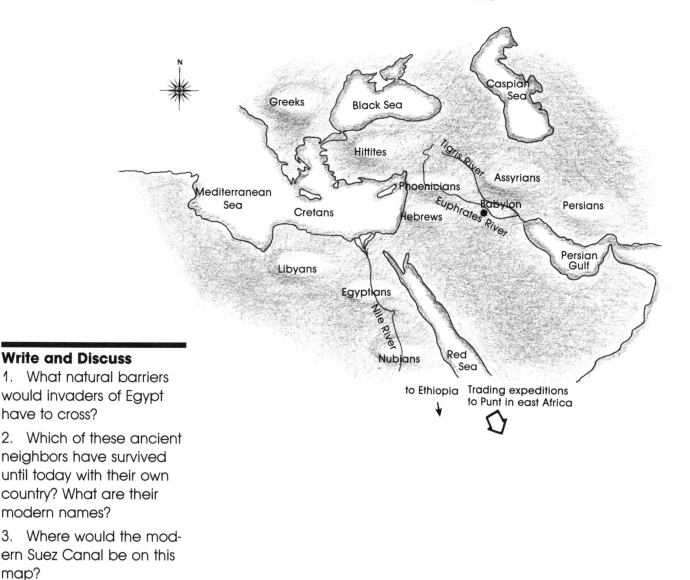

Write and Discuss

1. What natural barriers would invaders of Egypt have to cross?

2. Which of these ancient neighbors have survived until today with their own country? What are their modern names?

3. Where would the modern Suez Canal be on this map?

*An Assyrian **ziggurat**—an ancient brick tower of steps or with a spiral inclined plane. These towers were similar to the early Egyptian step pryamids.*

The Late Kingdom (656–332 BC)

Important pharaohs: Necho II, Psamtik III
Important events:

- Necho II begins a canal from the Nile to the Red Sea.

- Later, the Persians conquer Egypt and Pharaoh Psamtik III becomes the last native pharaoh of Ancient Egypt.

Write and Discuss

1. What is a dynasty of pharaohs?

2. What countries bordered Ancient Egypt (refer to the map)?

3. What raw materials did the Egyptians have to import from other countries?

4. What were the two main capital cities of Ancient Egypt?

5. What names are given to the periods of time when the power of the pharaohs faded and the country broke up into smaller units?

6. Find the following places on the map—Nubia, Kush, Punt. Why were they important places in the history of Egypt?

7. What inventions or improvements did the Hyksos kings introduce into Egypt? Can you explain why these improvements were important?

8. What were the names of some of the important gods of Ancient Egypt?

9. How many different types of invaders have taken over Egypt? What would have been the attraction for foreign attackers?

10. Tutankhamen was only about 18 when he died, but he is remembered more than any of the other pharaohs. Why do you think this is so?

Activity

The power of modern countries sometimes lasts for several hundred years. The British Empire was powerful for 200 years. France was a great power for over 100 years. Egypt was a great country for about 2,000 years.

Write a paragraph of 10–15 lines on the following topic—"Why Ancient Egypt remained an important country for so long." These are some of the points that you might consider in your paragraph.

1. The richness of the Nile River valley meant that Egypt did not have any disastrous droughts or famines.

2. With the Sinai Desert in the east and the Libyan Desert in the west, Egypt was hard to attack by land.

3. Egypt had a series of very able pharaohs who ruled the country well and were good army leaders.

4. Even though Egypt was taken over by other countries several times, the Egyptians absorbed these new rulers so that the new rulers themselves became Egyptians.

Egypt from 332 BC to the Present

332 BC–AD 200

- Egypt becomes a colony of the Greek and later the Roman empires. Huge quantities of wheat and gold are taken to Rome.

- Cleopatra becomes queen of Egypt during this period.

AD 640–1882

- Egypt becomes a Muslim state, mostly under the control of the Arab and Turkish empires.

AD 1882–1953

- Egypt falls under British rule because of the Suez Canal and Egypt's key geographic position.

AD 1953 to Present

- A series of revolutions makes Egypt an independent state for the first time since the ancient period.

The Cult of Death

Ancient Egyptians had a very strong belief in life after death. They were not afraid of death because they were confident of another life. They believed that the next life would be similar to this life. It was therefore necessary to take food and clothes. The rich people and the pharaohs acted on this belief by storing furniture, gold, and even slaves in their tombs for later use. The body was preserved for the next life by preserving it as a mummy. This method of preservation worked well in Egypt where the climate was dry and the graves were moisture-free.

We know how the embalmers worked on the dead bodies. A Greek writer named Herodotus has left us a record of the process of embalming:

Embalming Bodies—Egyptian Style

Embalming is a distinct profession. The embalmers, when a body is brought to them, produce specimen models in wood, painted to resemble nature, and graded in quality; the best and most expensive kind is said to represent a being whose name I shrink from mentioning in this connection [the god Osiris]; the next best is somewhat inferior and cheaper, while the third sort is cheapest of all. After pointing out these differences in quality, they ask which of the three is required, and the kinsmen of the dead man, having agreed upon a price, go away and leave the embalmers to their work.

The most perfect process is as follows: as much as possible of the brain is extracted through the nostrils with an iron hook, and what the hook cannot reach is rinsed out with drugs; next the flank is laid open with a flint knife and the whole contents of the abdomen removed; the cavity is then thoroughly cleansed and washed out, first with palm wine and again with an infusion of pounded spices. After that it is filled with pure bruised myrrh, cassia, and every other aromatic substance with the exception of frankincense, and sewn up again, after which the body is placed in natrum [a type of salt], covered entirely over, for seventy days—never longer. When this period, which must not be exceeded, is over, the body is washed and then wrapped from head to foot in linen cut into strips and smeared on the under side with gum, which is commonly used by the Egyptians instead of glue.

In this condition the body is given back to the family, who have a wooden case made, shaped like the human figure, into which it is put. The case is then sealed up and stored in a sepulchral chamber, upright against the wall.

When, for reasons of expense, the second quality is called for, the treatment is different: no incision is made and the intestines are not removed, but oil of cedar is injected with a syringe into the body through the anus which is afterwards stopped up to prevent the liquid from escaping. The body is then pickled in natrum for the prescribed number of days, on the last of which the oil is drained off. The effect of it is so powerful that as it leaves the body it brings with it the stomach and intestines in a liquid state, and as the flesh, too, is dissolved by the natrum, nothing of the body is left but the bones and skin. After this treatment it is returned to the family without further fuss.

The third method, used for embalming the bodies of the poor, is simply to clear out the intestines with a purge and keep the body seventy days in natrum. It is then given back to the family to be taken away.

Source: *Mummies—Death and Life in Ancient Egypt*, J. Hamilton Paterson and C. Andrews, Collins, London, 1978.

The process of burial for a phraoh or a rich person was an expensive business that lasted for several months. The steps of burial are shown in the following illustrations.

Write and Discuss

1. Why did the embalmers have three different kinds of embalming?

2. Are bodies embalmed today?

Activity

In your notebook under the heading "Six Steps in the Burial of a Pharaoh," write down a sentence for each of the pictures describing what is happening at each step of the funeral.

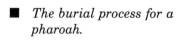

■ *The burial process for a pharoah.*

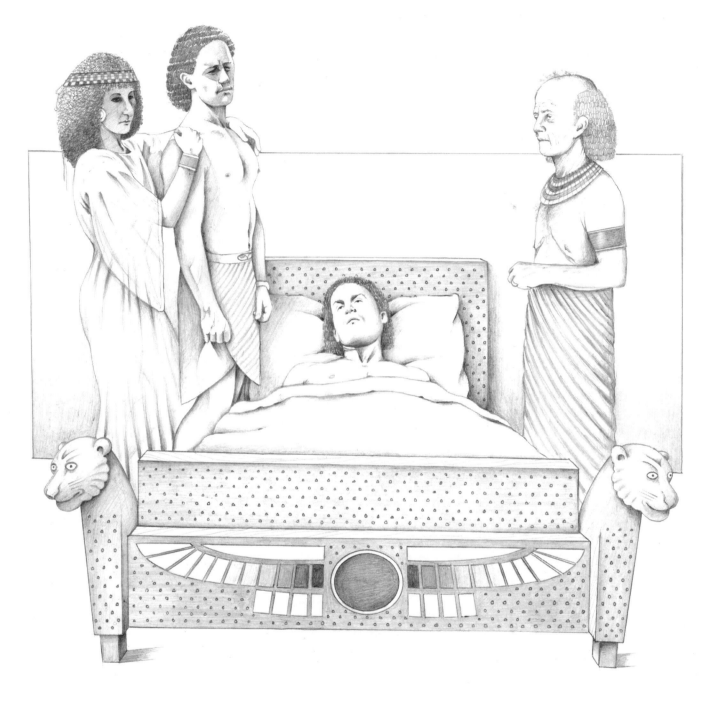

1. The Death of the Pharaoh.

The doctor can do no more. His master is dead. The pharaoh's first wife brings in the eldest son. He is to be the new pharaoh. He has to identify his father and confirm that the old pharaoh is dead. This is to prevent any future stories that the old pharoah is still alive or has been kidnapped.

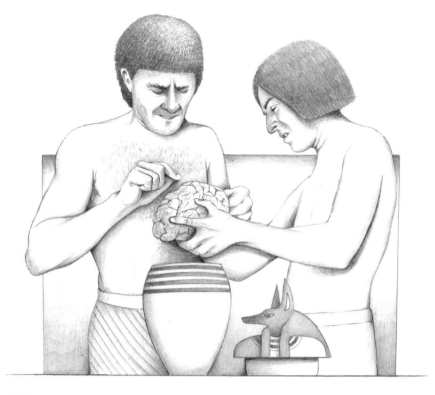

2.   The Embalmers at Work.
No time is lost. The embalmers have removed the heart, lungs, and liver. These are placed in special
jars that have the heads of gods depicted on their tops. These embalmers are very skilled. They
have cut open the head and removed the brain, which they are about to place in a special jar. These
jars will be placed in the tomb with the embalmed body of the pharoah.

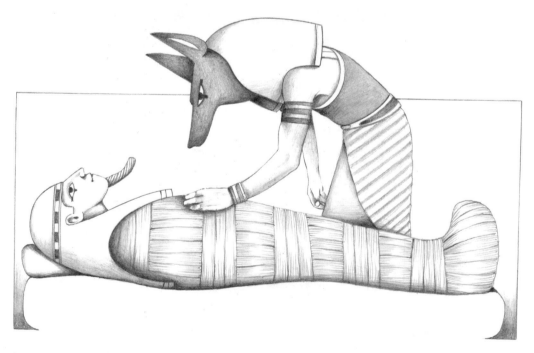

3.   Anubis Says Goodbye to the Pharoah's Mummy.
At least 40 days have passed (70 days according to Herodotus). The embalmers have spent long hours
wrapping the pharaoh's body in linen bandages. The body will be placed in several coffins shaped like
the pharaoh's body. Already a golden mask has been placed over the head. The chief priest has put
on the head of Anubis, the jackal god. This will be the first god that the pharoah will see in his new life.
Anubis (through the priest) is saying a last goodbye to the pharoah in this life.

4. The Royal Procession to the Tomb.

The pharoah is on his way to his new life. He has been ferried across to the west bank of the Nile, which is the Land of the Dead. Behind him are the official mourners. They must show great grief and sorrow. Behind the mourners is the chief priest. Then comes a long procession of all the pharoah's goods that will be buried with him in his tomb. The pharaoh's family, slaves, and officials walk along behind in this final journey.

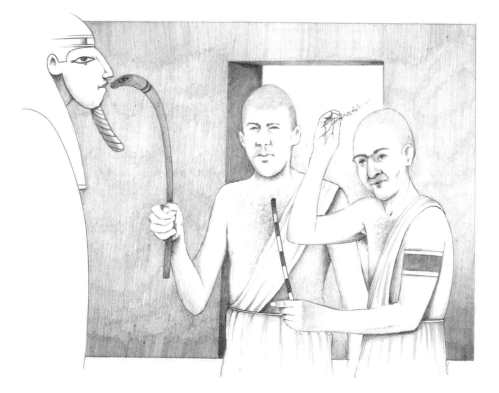

5. Opening of the Pharaoh's Mouth.

Inside the tomb the pharaoh's mummy is stood up like a living person. Up until now, the pharaoh has been dead, but his spirit must be released from the mummy. Then the spirit will live on until the day it will restore the pharaoh's body to full life. The priests are "opening the mouth." They are vitalizing the body for the future life.

6. The Final Goodbye.
The pharoah is carried into his secret tomb with all his wealth and furniture. The final prayers are said before the tomb is sealed up. Once this is done, no human signs must be left. The priest is sweeping away any footprints that may be on the floor. Powder or dust is sprinkled over the floor of the tomb and entrance passageways. If any robbers enter after the tomb is sealed, they will leave signs. The priests will make regular checks of the tomb entrance to make sure the pharoah is not disturbed. He must be left in peace if he is to be happy in the next world.

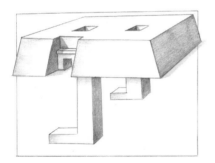

■ *A mastaba.*

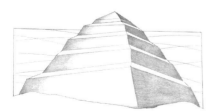

■ *A step pyramid.*

Tombs and Pyramids

Many buildings of the Ancient Egyptians have lasted all the years down to the present. The mud brick houses of the ordinary people have gone, but the stone buildings of the pharaohs have survived demolishers, earthquakes, and dynamite.

The first tombs were called **mastabas**. These were brick or stone buildings built over the tombs. Many of these were built as homes for the dead king. Bedrooms, bathrooms, and chapels were added. The builders always made sure there was a tiny window open to the outside world. The **ka** or spirit of the dead person would be free to come and go and keep contact with the body.

The pharaoh Djoser went one step farther. Instead of a plain mastaba, he built a step pyramid. Originally, these pyramids had a smooth coating of granite, limestone, or marble over the steps of the pyramid. This covering has been stripped off or fallen from the pyramids. The pharaohs built secret tunnels and rooms under the pyramids and inside the pyramids. These were to be the tombs of the pharaohs and they were frightened that tomb robbers would steal the valuable items from their tombs.

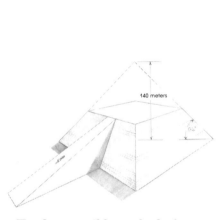

■ *One possible method of construction.*

■ *A pyramid with secret rooms and tunnels.*

At Giza, near Memphis, the pharaoh Khufu built the Great Pyramid of blocks of stone. Khufu's son erected the Great Sphinx next to the three pyramids at Giza.

Mysteries of the Pyramids

The first mystery of the pyramids is the accuracy of the building. The pyramids at Giza have walls that are almost perfectly even in length—the difference is only 8 cm (about 3 inches). The slope of the walls to the top is exactly $54°$. Some experts claim that there must have been some central post or pole for the builders to aim at. How else could the edges of the pyramid have met exactly at a point 148 meters—over 400 feet—in the air?

The second mystery is the way the builders moved the huge stones into position. The central core of the pyramids is local rock, but the outer layer is granite from Aswan, up the river. The builders probably floated the 2- to 30-ton blocks down the Nile River to Giza. They dragged the blocks (two million of them!) across the desert and levered them into position with wooden poles. It is not known how they managed to lift them to the upper levels. We know that early Egyptians did not use horses or wheeled wagons. They certainly did not have cranes that could lift 30 tons.

The illustration shows a method of construction that could have been used, but it would have taken a massive ramp to make it possible. A reasonable angle of incline would have been about $25°$. How long would such a stone and dirt ramp have to be to make the task possible?

The third mystery involves some of the details of building the pyramids. The modern stone mason needs at least 15–20 mm (less than an inch) of mortar to make a successful joint. However, the huge blocks of stone inside the tunnel of the Great Pyramid are joined together by joints that are accurate to one millimeter. It is difficult to believe that this could have been done using only hand chisels. The coffin of the pharaoh Khufu was placed in a huge stone container inside the tomb room. This stone container, or sarcophagus, is 5 cm (about 2 inches) wider than the tunnel that leads into the room. It is not known how the builders got the stone sarcophagus inside the tomb.

The Valley of the Kings

When the capital of Egypt was moved up the river to Thebes, the practice of building pyramids was changed. Instead, the pharaohs were buried in the Valley of the Kings, a stony desert valley west of the Nile. Many of these tombs are still hidden, safe from tomb robbers. Some of them have magnificent entrances carved out of the cliff face. Inside there are elaborate tunnels and secret rooms. Tutankhamen's tomb was found in this area in 1922.

The Gods of Ancient Egypt

The Ancient Egyptians were highly religious people. They lived close to the soil and were witnesses of the cycles of nature and the Nile each year. For this reason it is no surprise that many of their gods were closely related to the natural world of the sun and animals.

Many Egyptian gods took human form, and the pharaohs claimed to be children of certain gods. The Egyptians were believers in judgment after death and an afterlife. Some of their gods were therefore special gods related to death.

Although the Ancient Egyptians worshiped many gods and goddesses, their main god was Re, the Sun God of the Old Kingdom. Every day the god Re could be seen making his journey across the sky as the sun. Memphis was the center of Re's worship.

The ruler of the afterworld was Osiris, who was supposed to be the spirit of a murdered pharaoh. Osiris represented the hopes of resurrection for all future pharaohs.

Osiris's wife was Isis, the most important Egyptian goddess. Their son was Horus, who had the head of a falcon. It was Horus's task to welcome the dead person into the afterworld and present the person to Osiris for judgment.

At the judgment, Anubis, the jackal-headed god, weighed the heart of the dead person to decide whether that person could be accepted into the afterworld.

While Anubis weighed the dead person's heart, Thoth, the scribe god with the head of an ibis (a kind of bird), kept a record of the dead. Thoth's record was like the book of the dead that the priests recorded for people to take into the next life with them.

Write and Discuss

1. What are the names of the Egyptian gods in this picture?

2. What is the job of each god?

■ *Egyptian gods weighing the soul of a dead person.*

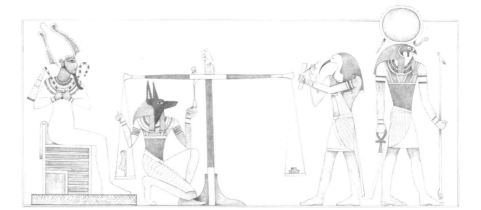

■ *The sun god Re making his daily journey across the sky. This explained the rising and setting of the sun every day.*

Egyptian Writing

We know a lot about the Egyptians by the paintings and statues they have left behind. Most of their drawings have been found in the cool, dry rooms of the tombs and underground temples.

As well as drawings, Egyptian writing has been preserved in these places, allowing historians to study it. The Egyptians were among the first people to develop a type of paper. This was made by peeling strips of the papyrus plant and hammering them into a coarse type of paper. This paper was plentiful so it was used for many purposes, from commercial accounts to letters.

Over the years the Egyptians used different types of writing. The most famous is **hieroglyphic writing**, which is picture writing. Although this picture writing seems at first glance to be simple, scholars have learned to read it only during the past hundred years.

Why is it difficult to read? The illustration shows the simplest form of hieroglyphic writing. Each picture or symbol stood for an object. There were over 700 of these to learn.

This form of writing was sufficient for writing about objects, but it became difficult to use if the writer wanted to write about ideas or complicated actions. The pictures were then combined to make a complex picture of the idea. This second, complicated form of hieroglyphics is very difficult to translate.

A third type of hieroglyphics was a system of sound signs, or **phonograms**, in which a picture stood for a sound. There were no pictures for the vowels *A, E, I, O, U*, nor were there signs for *V* or *J*. The diagram illustrates what the phonograms looked like.

The problem in translating hieroglyphics is that the Egyptians mixed the three methods of writing together. It is difficult to know when the writing changes from one form to another.

Since picture writing was not always convenient for quick messages, the Egyptians simplified the hieroglyphics into a running writing known as **hieratic**. In form it looks something like the cursive writing we use today.

After 700 BC, this hieratic writing was simplified even further into **demotic** writing, which was a wedge type of printing. Demotic writing was easy to carve on stone because of its lack of curves and its simple, sharp angles. So at this time, there were five different types of writing:

1. three types of hieroglyphics

2. simpler hieratic writing

3. even simpler demotic writing.

The problem for scholars was that they could not translate the Egyptian writing fully.

◤ The Rosetta Stone—The Answer to the Riddle

In 1799 French archaeologists discovered a black stone at Rosetta in Egypt. On it was written a tribute to the pharaoh, Ptolemy V, who ruled during the Greek dynasty (203–181 BC). The tribute was written in three scripts—Greek, demotic, and hieroglyphics. Scholars assumed that the three inscriptions were the same message. They could easily translate the Greek but could not match it with the hieroglyphics.

Finally, in 1822, a French scholar named Jean François Champollion was able to crack the code. He did it by comparing the pharaohs' names. He was able to isolate key letters and sounds of the alphabet and then unlock the rest of the message. One of the keys was the comparison between the two names of pharaohs that were known:

The three letters *P, T,* and *L* had been a mystery until the work of Champollion.

■ *Courtesy of The British
Museum.*

Activity

Here is a summary of the section on Egyptian writing. Some of the key words have been left out. These words are hidden deep in the pyramid puzzle. Several of the words are not mentioned in the text but as an Egyptologist, you will be able to find them in the pyramid.

■ **Remember:** *Egyptian tunnels are not always horizontal. There are vertical shafts as well as tunnels. There is even a sloping diagonal tunnel in this pyramid. See if you can find 10 words.*

Writing is one of the signs of a civilized society. It was no different for _____. Picture writing or _____ writing was the earliest form. It was often found written on the walls of _____. Because it was a complicated alphabet, a briefer running writing called _____ was developed.

For everyday writing Egyptians used _____, which was made from reeds growing in the river. A whole class of professional writers called _____ was employed to register necessary records, documents, and letters.

The discovery of the _____ stone made it possible to finally crack the code of the hieroglyphic alphabet. By working from the known writing, the French scholar _____ was able to _____ the original hieroglyphics. We are now more fully able to understand Egyptian _____ and the everyday life of the Egyptian common people.

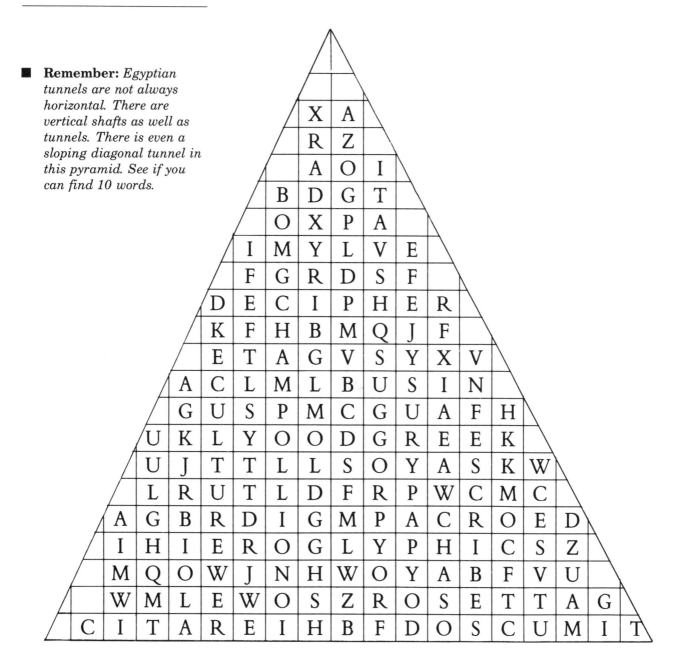

Life for the Common People

We know a lot about the pharaohs and their buildings but not a lot about the ordinary Egyptian people who lived out their lives as simple farmers and workers. Inside the pyramids of Giza there are scraps of graffiti that tell us something about the gangs of workers:

"Built by the fastest gang of the Nile"
and
"who can match our workers of Memphis"

These are two of the secret writings inside the pyramid tunnels. This tells us a little about the pride and competition of the ancient workers. They knew they were working on the greatest buildings in history. Now that we can translate hieroglyphics we can read some scraps that are written about the ordinary people.

■ *No one goes hungry on the Nile—everyone, including the peasants, had enough to eat from the Nile.*

Write and Discuss

What sorts of foods would the Egyptians enjoy by living along the Nile River?

A tribute to ordinary Egyptians was made in one of the nobles' tombs at Thebes. There is a painting of farmers on the Nile. Some are minding the ducks while others are digging in the garden. A poem beneath the picture was written in praise of the kind noble who let the people work for him, but some of the poem tells about the ordinary people. A similar poem is written below.

All people can live on the Nile,
The Nile is our life, above it,
beside it, below its waters.
Even the poorest peasant is
fed by our Nile.
The sun, the plants, the water,
the soil are always there.
No-one goes hungry, there is
                    enough for all.

While the lives of ordinary Ancient Egyptians may have been pleasant, the life of the common soldier seems to have been very hard. The following excerpt is from a text for schoolboys at a Theban school.

Write and Discuss

Is this excerpt in favor of army life or against it? Give reasons for your answer.

The Egyptian Soldier

Come, let me tell thee of the woes of the soldier! He is awakened when an hour has passed, and he is driven like an ass. He works till the sun sets. He is hungry, his body is exhausted, he is dead while yet alive.

He is called up for Syria. His marchings are high up in the mountains. He drinks water every three days and it is foul with the taste of salt. His body is broken with dysentery. The enemy comes, and surrounds him with arrows, and life is far away from him. They say, "Hasten on, brave soldier—win a good name for yourself!"—but he is barely conscious, his knee is weak and his face hurts him.

When the victory comes, His Majesty hands over the captives to be taken down into Egypt. The foreign woman is faint with marching, so she is placed on the neck of the soldier. His knapsack falls and others take it while he is loaded down with the Syrian woman. His wife and children are in their village, but he dies and never reaches it.

Source: *Red Land, Black Land*, Barbara Mentz, Hodder and Stoughton, London, 1967.

Write and Discuss

1. Draw a floor plan of a peasant's house.

2. Why do you think there was a wall around the house?

3. Why was the house whitewashed with lime?

4. In what ways was this house a suitable design for a hot desert region?

5. Can you suggest two reasons why the Egyptian house had a flat mud roof rather than a sloping roof?

6. Why would such a house design be unsuitable for many areas in the United States?

Houses of the Egyptian Peasants

The houses of ordinary people were simple and practical. Unlike the stone buildings of the pharaoh, a peasant's house was built of clay bricks. The clay bricks were made on the building site and dried in the sun. The house had strong wooden poles across the ceiling, and on top of these poles a mud roof was poured just like cement.

1. What precautions were taken so that the kings' tombs would not be robbed?

2. Would you like to be a builder of pharaohs' tombs? Give a reason for your answer.

3. In the confession the robber says he and his companions set fire to the king and queen's coffins. Below are four possible reasons why the robbers did this. Discuss these reasons and decide which reason seems to be the most likely.

The robbers burned the coffins because:

   a. They wanted to destroy their fingerprints.

   b. They wanted to hide their crime of stealing by destroying the interior of the tomb.

   c. They were vandals who enjoyed stealing, smashing, and destroying things.

   d. They felt that if they destroyed the king's body, the king could not punish them for the robbery.

Peasants' houses were designed for the climate. There was an outside upstairs patio for sleeping on hot nights. The windows were small to keep out the hot sun. Conelike buildings in the yard were used to store grain. The whole house was painted with a form of whitewash made from lime.

The Tomb Robbers

Robbing a rich person's tomb was a common practice in Ancient Egypt. Not only poor people became robbers. Some pharaohs robbed tombs to use the money and wealth. Usually such robbery was regarded as a serious crime because it meant that the dead person could not enjoy full happiness in the next life. However, this did not stop some people from robbing the rich graves.

By the time modern archaeologists came to Egypt searching for tombs, nearly all of the pharaohs' tombs had been robbed. That is why the discovery of Tutankhamen's tomb caused such a sensation. It was the only complete tomb to be found in modern times.

The pharaohs went to great pains to protect their tombs. Secret passages, execution of the tomb's architect, and threats of death were some of the steps they took. We do have a record of what happened to one group of tomb robbers. A pile of papyrus scrolls dating back to 1100 BC was found in a cave. The scrolls were court records of crimes. The following is the confession of a tomb robber who was caught. The robber and his companions were later executed.

> We broke through the tomb of the king [Sebekemsaf] in the rear chamber. We found the deep shaft and took torches in our hands and went down. We broke down the rubble wall, which we found at the mouth of the passage, and found the god lying at the back of his tomb, and we found the tomb of his queen, Nubkha"a . . . likewise. We opened their sarcophagi and their coffins . . . and found the noble mummy of the king with a scimitar. There were many amulets and gold jewels round his neck and he wore a mask of gold. The noble mummy of the king was completely covered with gold and his coffins were ornamented with gold and silver inside and out and inlaid with all kinds of precious stones. We collected the gold . . . and set fire to their coffins. We took the equipment which we found with them, objects of gold, silver, and bronze, and divided it amongst ourselves . . . twenty *deben* of gold fell to each of us.

Source: *Heritage of the Pharaohs*, John Ruffle, Plaidon Press Ltd. Oxford, 1977.

The Way the Egyptians Looked at Things

In drawing and painting, we have the problem of drawing things in **perspective** so that they look natural. We know that Egyptians looked at things differently because of the way they drew. Below are two drawings of a walled garden with a pool. The first is drawn in modern perspective, and the second is drawn in Egyptian fashion.

Write and Discuss

In what way is each drawing superior in what it shows the reader?

Write and Discuss

1. Why might all the soldiers of an army look the same in an Ancient Egyptian drawing?

2. Would it be easier or harder to paint in Egyptian times?

3. Do you think their way of drawing and painting is superior to the modern way? Do modern artists have "rules of proportion"?

When Egyptians drew people they drew them differently than we do today. Look at the pictures of two people walking past us. In what ways is the Egyptian perspective different from the modern view?

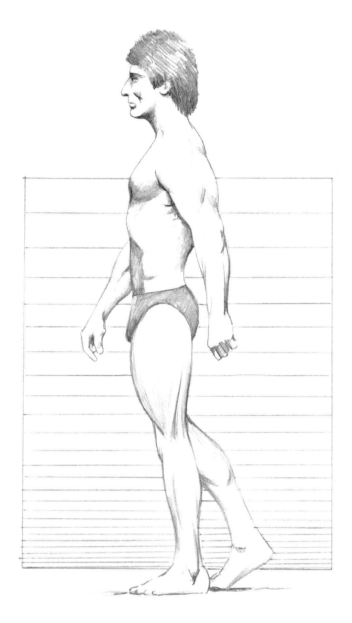

Over the past 50 years, half-finished wall paintings have been discovered in the Valley of the Kings. These wall paintings were left in the drawing stage, before the colored paint was added. The rough stone walls are plastered smooth with lime and sand plaster, and the walls are divided into squares. These paintings were probably only half done when the tomb had to be closed up.

In the incomplete paintings, the people and animals are all the same shape. The drawings suggest that the Ancient Egyptians had "rules of proportion" that determined how things had to look. They were not free to draw or paint differently.

Egyptians of the Twentieth Century

The people of Egypt today are descended from the first Egyptians of long ago. Since then, Egypt has had several invasions of other people. The first Egyptian people mixed with the invaders who marched in and took them over for a time.

6. During floodtime Ineek helped carry baskets of gravel and sand for the pharaoh's pyramid building.

In 525 BC, the Persians took over Egypt. By 332 BC, the Greeks had replaced the Persians. The Greeks were in turn replaced by the Romans who made Egypt a Roman colony by 30 BC. By AD 642, the Arabs from the East had succeeded the Romans as the new rulers of Egypt. Between 1517 and 1870, Egypt was part of the Turkish Empire.

Today there are 54 million people in Egypt. Cairo, the capital city on the Nile River, is home to 6 million people. Most of the people still live as farmers along the river. These farmers grow cotton, rice, and vegetables as their main crops. Modern Egyptians still use the shadoof for irrigation, as well as water wheels that lift water from the river. The sound of gasoline engine pumps also can be heard as they gush water onto the gardens. The farmers are now helped by the huge Aswan Dam upstream. This supplies them with water, even during the dry season.

Along the Nile the ancient dhow riverboats sail from the delta up the river to busy Cairo carrying vegetables from the delta region. Similar dhows sail down the Nile carrying clay water jars to the city for the workers to use as water coolers.

In Cairo there is the buzz of cars and motorcycles but ancient forms of transport are still used to carry goods. On the skyline of Cairo, the outlines of Moslem mosques remind us that 90 percent of the people are Moslem, or followers of Islam.

Since 1953, the Egyptian Republic has been involved in several wars against its neighbor, Israel. In 1979, Egypt's former President Sadat was responsible for a peace treaty with Israel over the territory of Sinai. This was a sign that Egypt was ready to make peace.

In 1956 Egypt took over control of the Suez Canal, which connects the Mediterranean Sea with the Red Sea. This canal and the export of cotton goods are the main sources of income for Egypt.

Activity

Here is a crossword puzzle for you to solve. In it are names of people, places, and things related to Egypt.

Across

2. A line of pharoahs of the same family.
4. The name for a king of Egypt.
6. They used these to pull the plows through the muddy fields.
7. They harvested this and stored it for use in the hungry periods.
8. An Egyptian word for the soul or the person's spirit double.
9. When horses were introduced into Egypt, these were used as war transport machines.
10. These riverboats still sail along the Nile.
11. They slept on this upstairs on hot nights.
14. The study that involves digging up ruins and learning about the past.
16. The bricks for Egyptian houses were made from _____.
18. The River Nile emptied into this sea.
19. This early pharaoh built the first step pyramid.

Down

1. When the river level fell, the farmers used _____ to water the crops.
3. This Greek king conquered the Middle East region and his generals set up a Greek dynasty of pharaohs.
5. An early form of Egyptian picture writing.
9. A river bird with long legs which often appeared on Egyptian wall paintings.
12. Either side of the Nile was a desert _____.
13. Every dead pharaoh and important person was converted into a _____ by embalmers.
15. The Great Pyramid of Khufu is found at _____.
17. Another word for the *dry* desert is the _____ desert.

Chapter Three

Israel

The Promised Land

 ## A Land of History

Like Egypt, Israel is in an area known as the Middle East. In relation to Europe, China and Japan were known as the Far East. The area in between Europe and Asia is still called the Middle East.

The land that is now called Israel has always been important, both in the ancient world and the modern world. Look at the map of modern Israel. Notice its geographic position compared with other countries. Several of the countries close to Israel were at some time powerful military states. (You have read about some of these in Chapter 2.) Because of its location between Egypt and other countries, such as Assyria, Persia, and Greece, Israel was involved in many invasions and military expeditions.

Today modern Israel is a Jewish nation surrounded by Muslim nations. This creates constant religious and political tension, and many incidents occur in the area that could flare up into war. Israel is also near the area where much of the world's oil is found. This makes the area very important to the rest of the world.

Israel is also important because it is the land of the Bible. It was from Israel that **Judaism** and **Christianity** developed and spread all over the world. It is also an important country in the history of **Islam**. In other words, three world religions, much Western law, and many customs began in Israel.

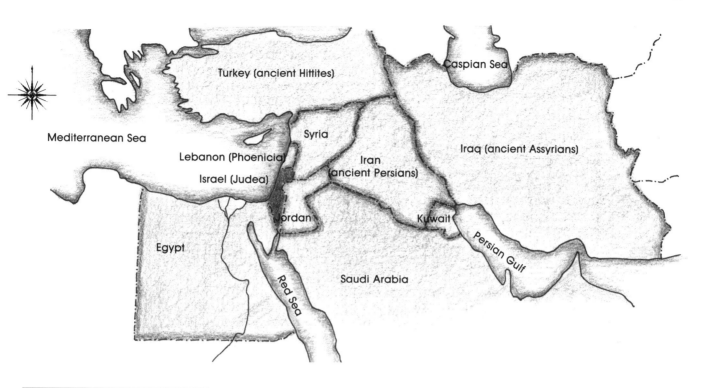

Activities

1. Read your local news-paper for one week. How many references to the Middle East or Israel can you find?

2. An important set of guidelines for living, the Ten Commandments, came from Ancient Israel. What are the Ten Commandments? How are the Commandments part of many modern Western laws?

Record of a Nation

We know something of Stone Age people from the tools they left behind. We know something of the Ancient Egyptian people from the buildings they left behind, as well as the pharaohs' funeral items and wall paintings.

The people of Israel were among the first to leave a complete history of their nation in written form. The Old Testament of the Bible is a record of the Jewish people. The Bible's main purpose was religious. It was a series of small books or scrolls describing the close links between God and the Hebrew people. In the Bible were written down the rules and customs that were the basis of Judaism.

The Bible also told the history of the Jewish people. The Bible was first written down on separate scrolls around 400 BC. Before then, scholars believe, Jewish law had been passed down by the religious leaders from generation to generation. In AD 70, Jerusalem, the Jewish capital, was destroyed and the Jewish people were deported by the Romans. They took copies of the scriptures with them to such places as Rome, Constantinople, Alexandria, and Carthage. Over the centuries, these books have been collected into one book and translated into many different languages. There has always been debate about how true modern Bibles are to the original books. After all the copies and translations over 1,900 years, there have been changes made, either by accident or on purpose.

Activity

Because the Bible is such an important book to so many people, scholars are very interested in the Dead Sea Scrolls. One reason the scholars study the scrolls is to make sure modern translations of the Bible are correct.

The Bible has been translated into many languages over thousands of years. Here are two translations from the First Book of Moses, or the Book of Genesis, chapter 50, verses 25 and 26. The first translation is a seventh-century Latin version. The second translation is a modern English version.

Latin Translation

"Colligetis assa mae hinc vobiscum et. Mortuus est Joseph cum esset annorum CX. Et saepeuerunt eum et posuerunt eum in sarcophagum in Aegyptum."

English Translation

"You will collect my bones and take them with you out of this place. Joseph died when he was 110 years old. They embalmed him and they placed him in a coffin in Egypt."

1. Are there any words that are the same between the Latin and English versions? Can you recognize any other words in the Latin version?
2. What are the Roman numerals that stand for 110?

■ *A Dead Sea Scroll. Courtesy of the Israel Museum, Jerusalem.*

Beginning in 1947, there was a remarkable series of discoveries in Palestine (an early name for what is now Israel). Arab shepherds discovered a collection of scrolls hidden in caves near the Dead Sea. The scrolls were written in the Hebrew language. The Dead Sea Scrolls had been sealed in the caves by Jews who lived as hermits in the desert caves. When the Romans came, the Jews hid their writings in the caves.

The Dead Sea Scrolls were checked with the modern Bible and were found to be very close in words and meaning. The Dead Sea Scrolls cover only about one-quarter of the total Bible. Scholars continue to study the scrolls carefully to better understand the history and teachings of the Bible.

The Bible is the main source of information about the Ancient Jewish people. In their early days they were wandering shepherds. Later, when they lived in Israel, their country and cities were destroyed several times, leaving few buildings or relics to help archaeologists. For hundreds of years the Hebrew people were prisoners in Egypt, Babylonia, and other places. Their story in the Bible is the only continuous record of their life as a nation. In this chapter we will follow that story and discover how important Israel was in the world's history.

To Egypt and Back

The Hebrews were originally a herding people. They lived like the Bedouin Arabs of recent history. They lived in the Fertile Crescent area of Sumer near the Euphrates River. About 2000 BC, these early Hebrews spread their area of herding across to the land of Canaan (what is now modern Israel). The Hebrews needed a large area of land to move their sheep, goats, and camels from area to area.

The land probably became exhausted from too much grazing, as the Hebrews took their flocks to Egypt during a drought around 1370 BC. The Bible mentions this period in the Book of Genesis:

> And Pharaoh said to Joseph "Say to your brothers, do this; load
> your beasts [with grain] and go back to the land of Canaan;
> and take your father and your households and come to me and
> I will give you the best of the land of Egypt, and you shall eat
> the fat of the land."
>
> Genesis 45: 17–18

The Hebrews lived in Egypt for about 80 years. By this time the Hebrews had become slaves in Egypt. The new pharaohs saw the Hebrews as a threat:

> "Behold the people of Israel are too many and mighty for us"
> Exodus 1: 9.

Moses, the leader of the Hebrews, led his people back to the Promised Land of Israel. In the 80 years that the Hebrews had been in Egypt, the land of Israel had recovered from the grazing of the sheep and goats. The Hebrew leaders always sent scouts ahead of the people to make sure there was enough grass and water for their traveling flocks. These scouts also kept a lookout for enemies or raiders that might be ahead. The scouts described what they saw as the "Land of Milk and Honey."

The Hebrew Tribes Become a Nation

When the Hebrews returned to Israel, they found that the Canaanites had occupied their Promised Land. The first task of the Hebrews was to win some of this territory. They did not hesitate to attack the Canaanites, and after a long series of battles the Hebrews were in control of most of the hill country.

When they fought, the Hebrews favored hit-and-run attacks and ambushes against the Canaanites. Small groups from each tribe were sent along to fight together but they were not a full-time army. In times of emergency a judge usually emerged as a popular leader who led the tribes in battle. After the fight the judge went back into the ranks of the people. The Hebrews had no leader—only their God.

The nation of Hebrews was very unusual. It was divided into 12 tribes that took their names from the sons of Jacob, the leader who had taken the Jews into Egypt. Each of these tribes had elders who sometimes met together. The thing that bound the tribes together was the Ark of the Covenant.

This Ark, or small temple, was carried around by the tribes in their wanderings. Inside it were the Ten Commandments carved in stone. The Ark meant a contract between the Jews and God. They would remain faithful to the one God and in return God would protect them as the "chosen people."

When they settled in Israel, the Hebrews built a bigger temple for the Ark of the Covenant at Shiloh, one of their hill towns. By now, the wandering Hebrews had become Israelites. They had put their tents away and had spread out as small farmers and herders.

Activities
1. What were the names of some of the neighbors of the Israelites?
2. See if you can find any information about the following towns and cities that appear on the map: Jericho, Bethlehem, Beersheba.
3. Jerusalem later became the capital city of Israel. With the help of an atlas, estimate where it would be on this map.

The Israelites and the Philistines

By 1050 BC, a new enemy began to replace the Canaanites. These were the Philistines, a people who had migrated from Cyprus. The Philistines had two advantages over the Israelites. First, they were allies of the Egyptian pharaoh, who used the Philistines to guard the highway to Egypt. Second, the Philistines had learned the art of making iron tools from the Hittites in the north. When the Philistines fought the Israelites, the bronze swords of the Israelites were no match for the iron spears and swords of the Philistines.

Even in peacetime the Philistines kept their iron smelting skills a secret. The Israelite farmers from the hills used to send their plows and harvesting sickles down to the coast to be repaired and sharpened

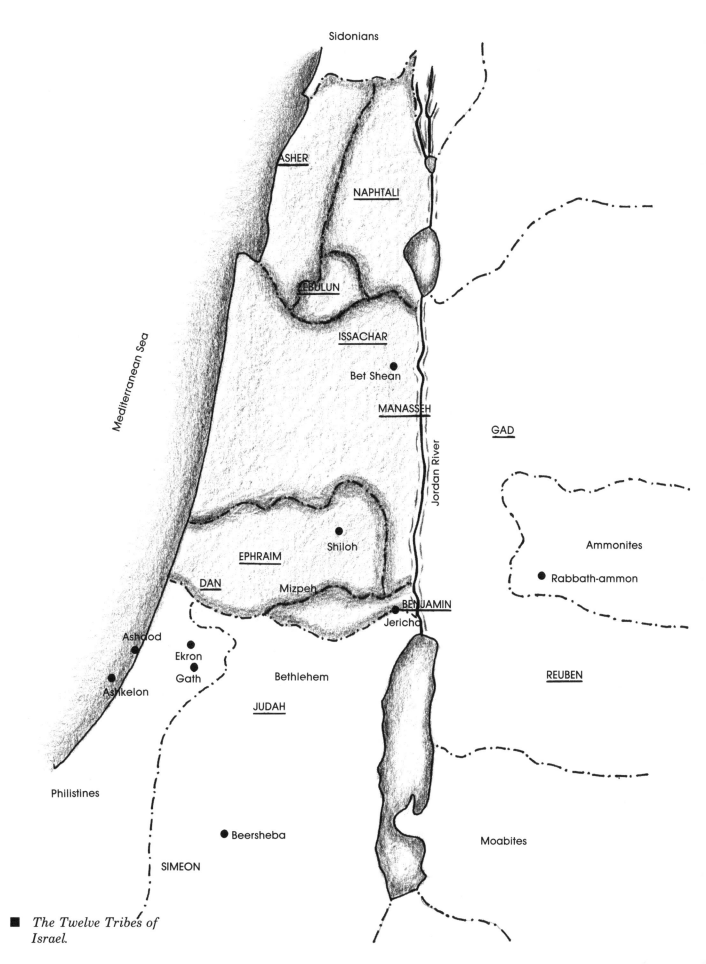

Sidonians

ASHER

NAPHTALI

ZEBULUN

ISSACHAR

• Bet Shean

MANASSEH

GAD

Mediterranean Sea

Jordan River

Ammonites

• Rabbath-ammon

Shiloh •

EPHRAIM

DAN

Mizpeh

• BENJAMIN

Jericho

REUBEN

• Ashdod

Ekron •

Gath •

Bethlehem

• Ashkelon

JUDAH

Philistines

• Beersheba

Moabites

SIMEON

■ *The Twelve Tribes of Israel.*

by the Philistines. The Philistines were prepared to sell iron farming equipment but not to show the Israelites how to make or repair iron tools.

The Israelites, with their guerilla war tactics, had no hope of capturing the strong cities of Gath and Ekron that belonged to the Philistines. The Israelites were against the idea of a human king but they realized that only by uniting under one king could they have a chance of defeating the Philistines.

A warrior was chosen from the Tribe of Benjamin. His name was Saul. He was anointed on the head with oil. This was a sign that he was chosen by God. (The same custom was repeated in 1953 at the coronation of Queen Elizabeth II of Britain.)

Saul worked for many years at defeating the Philistines. He was successful but died in battle before the final victory. Saul's place as king was taken by David. One of David's early tasks was to capture the city of Jerusalem. Jerusalem was a strongly walled city on a difficult ridge. It was placed directly between the southern tribes and northern tribes of Israel, which meant that it would make a perfect capital city for the united tribes. However, the city was defended by allies of the Philistines and seemed beyond the abilities of King David's lightly armed soldiers.

Problems Capturing Jerusalem

David and the Israelites faced several problems when they tried to capture Jerusalem.

1. The Israelites had no experience in the art of breaking into a walled city. They were open-desert fighters who used ambush and hit-and-run tactics rather than a long siege.

2. Jerusalem was perched up high so that the attackers would be in full view of the defenders. The Israelites did not have the numbers to take heavy losses.

3. The Israelites did not have siege machines or the mining skills to collapse the walls, which were built on solid rock.

4. The Israelites could make ladders and climb over the walls, but with no armor to protect them, their losses would be too high.

5. David could surround the city and cut off any supplies into Jerusalem. However, Jerusalem could probably hold out longer than the Israelites could afford to wait. In the first place, the Israelite army was needed back home for the harvest. In the second place, disease often broke out in a besieging army that had to live for long periods in camps that had poor sanitary conditions.

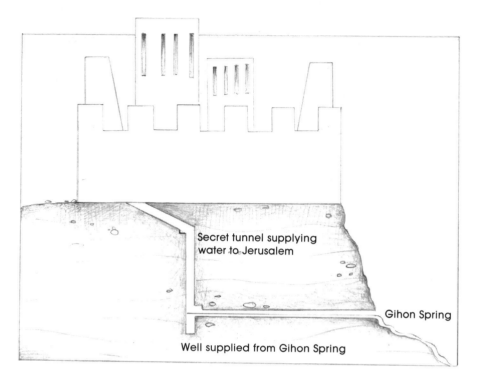

Secret tunnel supplying
water to Jerusalem

Gihon Spring

Well supplied from Gihon Spring

■ *The water supply for*
Ancient Jerusalem.

David was a clever leader. He knew there had to be a way to capture the city. He sent spies into Jerusalem. They reported back to him on the city's water supply. This was the weak point of the city.

David sent scouts into the tunnel that brought water into Jerusalem from the Gihon Spring. Two daring climbers climbed the shaft to the sloping tunnel. Soon a small group of Israelites were able to open a city gate and allow the rest of the army in. David's army captured the city of Jerusalem.

David was kind to the citizens of Jerusalem. They had the choice of leaving or staying in the city. If they accepted the God of Israel, the Jerusalem citizens would be accepted as Israelites.

David led a great march into Jerusalem. The Ark of the Covenant was carried into the city and there it was given a permanent home. The northern tribes and the kingdom of Judah (refer to map) were now united. Jerusalem became the political and religious center for all the tribes.

King David spent the rest of his life fighting wars and expanding the borders of Israel. At this time Egypt was weak and divided. This gave Israel a chance for a short period of history to build an empire from the Red Sea to the Euphrates River. Their control spread northward to Phoenicia (Sidon on the old map).

The Temple of Jerusalem

About 965 BC King David died and was replaced by King Solomon, his son. Solomon was a great trader and builder. He expanded on all the work done by his father. Solomon built the temple at Jerusalem to house the Ark of the Covenant. The new temple was a big step up from the tent that covered the Ark when it was carried from tribe to tribe. Now it was said that God did not move around the country but lived in only one place on earth—the temple in Jerusalem.

Solomon took 13 years to build the temple. Thirty thousand laborers were sent to Lebanon in the north to cut down and saw cedar. One hundred fifty thousand men worked in Jerusalem cutting out the limestone for stone blocks. Skilled stonemasons from Phoenicia were imported to cut the blocks of stone square the straight. Expeditions were sent to Africa for ivory and to India for gold.

In Solomon's time, the temple was one of the wonders of the world. It was to last almost 400 years. It was so richly decorated that it would have been a prize for any invader. Eventually, this is what happened. All its riches were torn down and carried off by the Babylonians in 586 BC.

■ *King Solomon's Temple in Jerusalem. The procession is carrying the Ark of the Covenant. This temple was destroyed by King Nebuchadnezzar of Babylonia. Most of the Israelites were taken as slaves back to Babylonia.*

The Decline of the Hebrew Nation

The kingdom of David and Solomon was the high point of the Hebrew nation. Not until the twentieth century would Israel again be a united Hebrew nation.

After Solomon's death the northern Israelites broke away from southern Judah and the two states fought a civil war for 50 years. Once the kingdom was broken up into two sections, outside invaders attacked the separate tribes and states. The first of these invaders were the Assyrians from the northwest. In 701 BC, King Sennacherib conquered the Hebrews. He took 25,000 captives into exile back to Assyria.

In his capital city of Nineveh, Sennacherib erected a stone carving of his victory. The message on the carving translates as follows:

> I, Sennacherib, King of Kings, took the field against the proud Hezekiah. Hezekiah was helped by the Egyptians who sent an army beyond counting, but I inflicted a defeat upon all of them.
>
> Hezekiah I made a prisoner like a bird in a cage in his palace. . . . I destroyed his country but I still increased the tribute to be paid annually.
>
> Hezekiah himself did send to my lordly city of Nineveh 30 talents of gold, 800 talents of silver, all kinds of valuable treasure together with his own daughters, concubines, and musicians.

In 586 BC, the Babylonian king Nebuchadnezzar defeated the Hebrews who had rebelled against him. He destroyed Jerusalem, including the temple, and carried off most of the citizens to Babylonia. Here they stayed in exile for 47 years.

In 539 BC, Cyrus of Persia captured Babylonia and allowed the exiles to return to their homeland. Jerusalem was slowly rebuilt but it was still the city of only the southern Hebrews of Judah. The northern Hebrews, who were called *Samaritans*, were banned from Jerusalem. They were regarded as heretics or traitors to the Jewish faith because they had obeyed the invaders and had not fought like the Judeans.

The next invasion of Israel was the Greek invasion. In 331 BC, Alexander the Great conquered Israel and deported many Hebrews out of their country.

In 63 BC, Roman soldiers marched into Jerusalem. Israel became a Roman colony with a Roman governor in Jerusalem. The Roman army was kept in Israel to keep the rebel Hebrews down. The Hebrews were always looking forward to their freedom. In the Bible the prophets, such as Isaiah, often promised freedom from foreign control. The Hebrews remembered how Moses had led them back from Egypt. They remembered how they were allowed to come home from their captivity in Babylon. The Jews hoped that one day a liberator or redeemer would come again to free them from Roman rule.

Write and Discuss

1. In Sennacherib's carving, what does the phrase "took the field" mean?
2. What was the "tribute" that Sennacherib increased?
3. See if you discover what "talents" were. What is unusual about the treasure that Hezekiah sent to Sennacherib?

King Sennacherib of Assyria judges a Hebrew captive after capturing Jerusalem in 701 BC.

 The Captivity of Israel

The high point of Israel's power was in the years of King David (1000–965 BC) and King Solomon (965–922 BC). For the rest of Israel's long history, invaders have occupied the land or carried off the Israelites as prisoners to another land. Following is a summary of Israel's history after the death of Solomon:

922–720 BC   Israel is divided into two warring kingdoms—southern Judah and northern Israel.

Write and Discuss

Look back at the map of Israel at the beginning of the chapter.
1. Why do you think Israel was regarded by invaders as a prize to be captured?
2. How was its geographic position important to other countries?

701 BC	The Assyrians under King Sennacherib defeat the Hebrews and carry 25,000 hostages back to Assyria.
586 BC	King Nebuchadnezzar of Babylonia destroys Jerusalem and takes most of the citizens to Babylonia.
331 BC	The Greek army occupies Israel and deports many Hebrews.
63 BC	The Roman army occupies Jerusalem. The city of Jerusalem is destroyed by the Romans in AD 70 and most of the Hebrews are sent into exile.

The Beginning of Christianity

During the Roman occupation of Israel, the Hebrew Jesus Christ was born in Bethlehem. Jesus was seen by many as the messiah—the liberator they had been waiting for. King Herod of Jerusalem was the Jewish king who ruled for the Romans. He heard about this messiah being born and called in his scholars and wise men. He saw the new liberator as a possible threat to his power as the leader of the Jews. He asked the scholars where the messiah was to be born. They increased his fears by quoting a prophecy made by Micah hundreds of years before:

> And you O Bethlehem, in the land of Judah,
> Are by no means the least among the rulers of Judah
> for from you shall come a ruler
> who will govern my people Israel.
>
> Micah 5: 2

Herod tried to kill the messiah by ordering all male babies to be killed in the Bethlehem district. He missed killing Jesus because Jesus' parents, Mary and Joseph, took their son to Egypt until the killing had ended.

Later, when Jesus was taken to the temple as a baby, a man called Simeon and a prophet named Anna announced that Jesus was the one they were waiting for:

> For mine eyes have seen thy salvation which thou has prepared
> in the presence of all peoples,
> a light for revelation to the Gentiles and for glory to thy people
> Israel.
> Behold this child is set for the fall and rising of many in Israel.
>
> Luke 2: 30–32, 34

During Jesus' life many people listened to his teachings about love and forgiveness. Many followed Jesus because they saw him as a possible new Saul or David who could lead them to victory over the

Write and Discuss

1. Why was King Herod worried when he heard about Jesus' birth?

2. Many of Jesus' teachings had to do with love and forgiveness. He taught that people should treat one another as they wished to be treated by others, and that people should not fight back when attacked. Why might these teachings have appealed to people who came to listen to him? Why might these teachings have seemed dangerous?

Romans. However, most of the Jews did not see Jesus as the messiah or liberator. They saw Jesus as a troublemaker who was going to make their life under the Romans even harder. The Romans also saw Jesus as a troublemaker. They did not want to risk an uprising against their rule.

In AD 33, Jesus was arrested for treason against Rome. He was accused of proclaiming himself "King of the Jews." Jesus was sentenced to death by the Roman governor and was executed by crucifixion (hanging on a cross).

With Jesus' death died the hope of relief from the Romans for many Jews. However, some of Jesus' followers continued to believe in his teachings. They believed that Jesus was resurrected (brought back to life) and that this meant the Kingdom of God was coming soon. These followers became the early Christians. They spread Jesus' teachings and the story of his life far beyond Israel.

The End of Ancient Israel

In the first century AD, the Jews became more and more restless under the Romans. One group of Jews wanted to keep peace with the Roman occupiers. Another group wanted to fight the Romans and expel them from Israel. These Jews were called **Zealots**. The word *zealot* has come into the English language to mean "very eager; almost fanatical." The original Zealots saw the Romans as a stain or blot on their land, so in AD 66 the Zealots and other patriots rebelled against their Roman masters.

The rebellion lasted until AD 70. The Roman general Titus destroyed Jerusalem and expelled the Jewish survivors from Israel. About 1,000 Zealots and their families retreated to the rock of Masada in the desert. Here they defied the Romans for two years, making raids on the Roman camps and raiding Roman food supplies.

The Roman general Silva was sent with the Roman Tenth Legion to destroy the hill fortress. The Romans tried to starve the Zealots out but they had large supplies of food and water. The fortress walls on top of the rock were impossible to attack from below. The Roman general used thousands of Jewish prisoners of war to build a long, earthen ramp 400 meters (over 1,000 feet) high on one side of the rock of Masada. This took several months to build. The Roman army then brought up battering rams and siege machines to the walls of the fortress. The Romans burned down a protective wooden fence and got reach to attack the fortress.

The Zealots had a mass meeting that night. They knew the Romans would attack at dawn. The writer Flavius Josephus has left a record of what happened to the Masada defenders:

Activities

1. This fortress was the country fortress of King Herod of Jerusalem. Who was King Herod?

2. What were the scrolls that were later found in the Masada fortress?

3. Before they died, the Zealots drew lots to decide who would be the 10 men to kill all the other members of the community. Find the place on the plan where this was decided. (You will need to read the story in the text before you answer this question.)

None of the Zealots hesitated to act their part in this terrible execution. Each man killed his own family. What a choice these sorrowing fathers had—to kill or be killed.

After each father had killed his family they lost no time in killing themselves. First they collected all they owned and burned it in one big heap. By lot, 10 men were chosen to kill all the surviving men. Every other man lay down by his dead wife and children and stretched out his neck. The 10 chosen Zealots went among their friends, cutting off the heads of the family leaders.

When this was done only the 10 men were left. One of them quickly killed the other 9. The sole survivor checked that everyone was really dead and then set fire to all the buildings. He then threw himself on his sword—the last Zealot to die.

So all these people bravely died; they would not give the Romans the pleasure of capturing even one of them.

Altogether that night 960 men, women, and children committed suicide. It was the fifteenth day of the month.

The next morning the Roman army burst in through the walls. They were met by a deathly silence. The Zealots were lying in family groups inside the fortress. Only two women and three children somehow survived to tell the story. The Romans were to have no triumph, no victory. They went away shaking their heads in disbelief at people who would do such a thing.

■ *The plan of the Zealots' fortress on top of the Masada.*

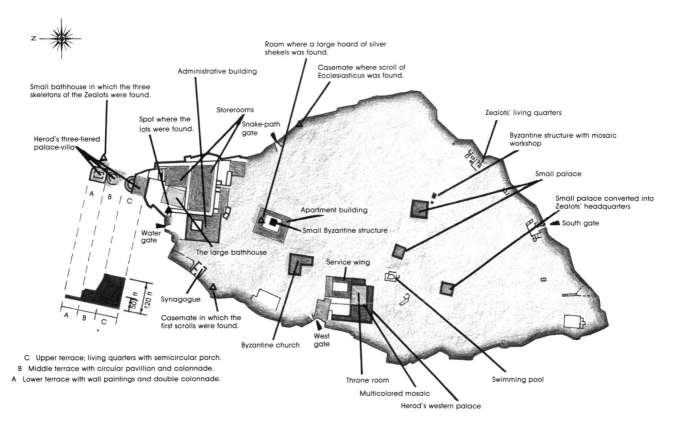

C Upper terrace; living quarters with semicircular porch.
B Middle terrace with circular pavillion and colonnade.
A Lower terrace with wall paintings and double colonnade.

Write and Discuss

1. Why did the Masada Zealots kill themselves?

2. Here are some other options that the Zealots could have taken:

(a) surrendered to the Romans in the morning.

(b) fought on but surrendered when it became hopeless and their families were in immediate danger.

(c) fought on to the last person and killed some Roman soldiers in the process.

What are the advantages and disadvantages of these options? Do you think the Zealots' actions were wise? Why?

3. Why do you think the Roman soldiers would have left the scene shaking their heads?

■ *A Roman soldier discovers the dead at Masada.*

The Legacy of Ancient Israel

After AD 70, the importance of Israel declined. The Jews were spread through North Africa, Turkey, Greece, and Italy. Only in the twentieth century did the Jews once more have an independent state of Israel.

The Jews have, however, had a great influence on Europe and much of the world. Their ideas have affected the way many people think about things. The following are some of the ideas that have come down to the modern world from the Ancient Israelites and their writings in the Bible.

1. There is one God who is an unseen spirit.

2. God cares for people and people obey God's law to please God.

Activity

Many Western ideas and ways of looking at life are influenced by sayings or proverbs in the Bible. Write down the meaning of each of these proverbs. Do they make sense today? Are they worth following as rules of living?

- Pride comes before a fall.
- He who spares the rod spoils the child.
- A grey-haired head is a crown of glory.
- He who lives by the sword dies by the sword.
- A fool and his money are soon parted.

3. There is a divine law that must be obeyed.

4. Each person is important with a special worth. All people are responsible to themselves and God for what they do.

5. God's law is superior to that of kings, and people have the duty and right to disobey a wicked king or law.

New Testament Ideas

The New Testament is the part of the Bible written after the death of Jesus. It concentrates on the life and teachings of Jesus and is the basis for the Christian religion. These are some of the ideas expressed in the New Testament:

1. You must love all people as well as God and yourself.

2. God is a God of love and forgiveness, not a God of judgment and punishment.

3. God is meant for all people, not just one group or nation.

The early Christians spread from Israel to Greece and Rome. They taught about Jesus and were often killed or imprisoned for their beliefs. However, by AD 350, Christianity had become the main religion of the Roman Empire.

The Twilight Years of Israel

The centuries between the Roman occupation of Israel and the twentieth century are sometimes referred to as the "twilight years." Although Jerusalem remained the holy city for all Jews, the Jewish people did not control it. Some of the Jewish people remained in Israel, but others scattered throughout the Middle East, Asia, and Europe. Israel was no longer a Jewish nation.

In the seventh century, Arab Muslims took over the whole area. For 300 years the Muslims controlled Jerusalem. They built places of worship (mosques) in the city. The **Muslims** believed in one God, Allah. Their religion, Islam, was built on Christianity and on the Jewish faith. Jerusalem was also a holy city for them.

In 1071 the Muslim Turks took over from the Arabs. These Turks were religious fanatics. They killed many Jews and Christians in Jerusalem. In response to the persecution of the Christians, European leaders sent Crusades to recapture Jerusalem. The first Crusade was in 1096. By 1099, the Crusaders had captured the city.

In 1187, the Muslim leader Saladin recaptured Jerusalem. Israel became part of the Turkish Ottoman Empire in the thirteenth century. Until World War I, it was under Turkish rule.

During World War I, the British army captured Jerusalem from the Turks. The question now was what to do with Israel. There were different groups claiming the right to control Israel, including the Jews who had lived there for 3,000 years. The problem was to decide whose country it was. The British government decided to control Israel itself until a final decision could be made.

Israel Reborn

Jews have always dreamed of Jerusalem and the Holy Land of Israel. It is their religious home in the same way that Mecca is for Muslims or Rome for Roman Catholics.

In the past hundred years, a new Jewish idea of Zionism has developed. This is the belief that Jews should return to Israel to set up a Jewish State of Israel. Until 1917, the Turks stopped this from happening; then the British army prevented the Jews from setting up an independent state.

During World War II millions of Jews were killed by the Nazis in Europe. This helped the idea of Zionism. After 1945 streams of Jews began returning to Israel. The British agreed to allow the Jews to set up the new State of Israel in 1948.

Since then there has been a mass migration to Israel. The city of Jerusalem has been rebuilt and modernized. The desert of Israel has been recovered to make new farms and orchards. Israel is full of energy and hope.

But there are two clouds spoiling the bright future of Israel. First there are the Arabs of Israel. They are called *Palestinian Arabs*, from the days when the area was called Palestine. Many of these Arabs have lived in the area for hundreds of years. They have not been given equal citizenship with the Israeli Jews. They claim that the Jews are squeezing them out of Israel. They want equal rights with Jews or to be allowed to set up their own independent state in the area of Palestine. Many Israelis do not want this because they fear the Arabs could be a threat to the Jewish State of Israel.

Activities

In the "twilight years," 1,700 years of Israel's history have been touched upon. Several of these sections are most interesting to study in more depth. The way to do this is to use general textbooks or an encyclopedia. Use the index to look up people and events connected with the topic. Here are some topics that you could research.

1. **The Roman Defeat of Israel (63 BC–AD 135)**
   - Herod—king of Israel.
   - Masada—fortress of Herod, later used by the Zealots.
   - Pontious Pilate—Roman governor of Jerusalem.
   - Zealots—freedom fighters of first century.

2. **The Arab Muslim Occupation of Israel**
   - Muhammed—the founder of the Islamic religion.
   - Islam—the new religion established in Israel.
   - Turks–Seljuk—the new wave of Muslim invaders who persecuted Christians in the eleventh century.

3. **The Crusades**
   - Crusades—the army expeditions from Europe to capture Jerusalem.
   - Pope Urban II—called for the Crusades.
   - Peter the Hermit—preached the Crusades through Europe.
   - Godfrey de Bouillon

and Tancred—famous leaders of the Crusaders.

- Saladin the Saracen—recaptured Jerusalem and defeated the Crusaders.
- Richard I (the Lion-Hearted)—famous English leader of one of the Crusades.

4. **The British Capture Jerusalem from the Turks (1917)**

- Allenby—the British general who led the British army into Jerusalem.
- Lawrence of Arabia—the British leader of Arabs who fought for Arab rights in Jerusalem.
- Chaim Weizmann—leader of the Jews during this period.

Write and Discuss

The new State of Israel has many questions and conflicts that have not been fully decided. See if you can come up with some answers to the following questions:

1. Do the Palestinian Arabs living in Israel have any right to be there or have a say in Israel?

2. How can the Jews give the Arabs in Israel an equal say without losing control of the country once again?

3. How can the hatred and distrust between the Arab countries and Israel be lessened?

The second cloud to darken the sky is the threat of Arab states around Israel. If you look at the map of the Middle East, you will find that Israel is surrounded by Muslim Arab states, such as Iraq, Iran, Lebanon, Syria, Egypt, Libya, and Jordan. These Muslim countries do not like the idea of the Jews controlling Palestine. In 1948, 1956, 1967, and 1973 there have been short, violent wars between some of these Arab states and Israel. Israel has been successful in all these wars and has increased the area of Israel by capturing more Arab territory. It is very difficult for these Arab states to make peace with Israel. There is the constant fear of future war.

The Jews have had many setbacks and disasters in the past. It is not likely that they will surrender any territory or allow the Arabs to pressure them out of Israel again.

- *An Israeli conscript soldier. Israel conscripts both men and women into its citizen army. This army is on call for security within Israel or possible defense or attack against unfriendly Arab neighbors.*

■ *The old city of Jersualem.*

Legend		
1. Indian Hospice	16. Coptic Patriarchate	31. Maronite Monastery
2. Church of St. Anne	17. Coptic Monastery	32. Christ Church
3. Monastery of the Flagellation	18. St. John's Hospice	33. St. Mark's House
4. Sisters of Zion	19. Church of St. Veronica	34. Chafetz Chayim Yeshiva
5. Antonia	20. Islamic Orphanage	35. Hurva Synagogue
6. Ecce Homo Arch	21. Church of the Redeemer	36. Ramban Synagogue
7. Austrian Hospice	22. Mosque of Omar	37. Habad Yeshiva
8. Red Mosque	23. Greek Monastery	38. Armenian Patriarchate
9. Polish Hospice	24. Casa Nova Hospice	39. Armenian Seminary
10. Ethiopian Monastery	25. Christian Brothers	40. St. James's Cathedral
11. Terra Sancta College	26. Latin Patriarchate	41. Church of St. George
12. Church of St. Savior	27. Greek Catholic Patriarchate	42. Four Sephardi Synagogues
13. Church of St. Michael	28. Church of St. George	43. Yeshiva Porat Yosef
14. Greek Orthodox Patriarchate	29. Hezekiah's Pool	44. Islamic Museum
15. Church of the Holy Sepulcher	30. Church of St. John the Baptist	45. Al Aksa Mosque

Activity

Here is a map of the Old City of Jerusalem. The Old City is now only a small part of the greater city of Jerusalem. Try to answer the following questions.

1. What evidence is there on the map that several major religions own holy places in Jerusalem?

2. Where is the Gihon Spring? Why was it important in the history of Jerusalem?

3. How many different countries have churches or property in Jerusalem? What are the countries' names?

4. Where on the map is the smaller city that King David built?

5. Are there any places on the map that have a connection with the life of Jesus?

6. Why were walls built around the Old City? Why are there so many gates to the city?

7. Some of the roads out of Jerusalem lead to other well-known cities. What are those roads?

8. An important part of the Old City in the Muslim section is the Dome of the Rock. It is a huge, dome-shaped building built over a rock that is regarded as holy by the Muslims. See if you can discover the significance of the Dome of the Rock.

Chapter Four

Greece

Land of Heroes

The Importance of Greece

If you look at a map of the Mediterranean area, you will see that Greece is in a central position. In ancient times the civilizations of China and India developed separately from Europe. In the Middle East area there were the Persians, the Egyptians, and the Hebrews of Israel.

Greece was the link between Western Europe and the East. Greece includes all the Greek islands of the Aegean Sea. The Greeks were great sailors and traders. They made contact with Egypt, Persia, and Israel. From the Middle East the Greeks adopted ideas and inventions. Greek traders later moved to Sicily and Italy where they spread their ideas. The powerful Romans learned from the Greeks.

The Romans spread their empire over the whole of Western Europe. So, indirectly, many ideas and crafts came to the modern world through the Greeks. They were in the right place at the right time to be the carriers of civilization.

One example of how the Greeks adopted and spread ideas is the modern alphabet. If you look at the alphabet table, you will see that the Modern European alphabet has developed from the Greek alphabet. The very early Greek traders traded with the Phoenicians, who

Write and Discuss

1. What letters do we use in the modern alphabet that were not in the Greek or Phoenician languages?

2. What letters might the Greeks use to make the sounds of the missing Greek letters in our alphabet, such as *C* and *Q*?

3. Are there any letters that the modern alphabet seems to have borrowed from the Greek only, or from the Phoenician alphabet only?

4. You wish to send a secret telegram to your friend. Write down the message in Phoenician or Greek. See if your friend can decode it.

Note: If you need a letter that doesn't exist in the Greek or Phoenician alphabets, just leave it out. The original Phoenician language did not have letters for the vowels *a, e, i, o, u*. The Phoenicians spoke the vowel sounds, but they did not write them down.

lived just north of Israel where Lebanon is now situated. The Phoenicians had an early alphabet, developed about 1000 BC. Look at the alphabet table and compare the languages.

Phoenician alphabet 1000 BC	Primitive Greek alphabet 800 BC	Classical Greek alphabet 200 BC	Modern European alphabet
		A — Alpha	a — A
		B — Beta	b — B
			c — C
		Δ — Delta	d — D
		E — Epsilon	e — E
			f — F
		Γ — Gamma	g — G
		H — Eta	h — H
		I — Iota	i — I
			j — J
		K — Kappa	k — K
		Λ — Lambda	l — L
		M — Mu	m — M
		N — Nu	n — N
		O — Omicron	o — O
		Π — Pi	p — P
			q — Q
		P — Rho	r — R
		Σ — Sigma	s — S
		T — Tau	t — T
		Υ — Upsilon	u — U
			v — V
			w — W
		◌ — Xi	x — X
			y — Y
		Z — Zeta	z — Z
		Θ — Theta	th — Th

Legend or History?

Every nation has legends of how their people started. These stories are passed down from generation to generation. The English have legends of King Arthur and the Knights of the Round Table. The Australian Aborigines have legends of the Dreamtime. The Greeks also had legends of their earliest times. These legends were written down by the Greek poet Homer between 800 and 700 BC. Homer wrote two books, the *Iliad* and the *Odyssey*. In the *Iliad* Homer tells the story of the city of Troy and the Greek attack on Troy. This was a favorite story of the later Greeks, but most people thought it was just a story. Here is the legend.

There was a king of Sparta named Menelaus who had a beautiful wife named Helen. One day a trading ship arrived from Troy with a handsome young prince of Troy named Paris. (This is where the story changes, depending on who is telling it.)

Version One: Helen fell in love with Paris and eloped with him on his trading ship back to Troy.

Version Two: Paris kidnapped Helen, wife of Menelaus, and sailed back to Troy with her as prisoner.

The Greeks sent messengers to Troy to try and get Helen back but—

Version One: Helen refused to return to her husband, King Menelaus.

Version Two: Paris refused to let her go home.

The Greek king at Mycenae got together all his allies from Sparta, Crete, and Athens. An invasion fleet sailed to Troy to capture the city and rescue Helen. In fact, Helen was probably a good excuse for the Greeks to attack Troy. The Greeks knew that Troy was a wealthy city with lots of treasure.

The Greeks could not capture the city of Troy. They stayed camped on the beach for nearly 10 years. They built huts on the beach and a wall to protect their ships.

The siege of the city was at a stalemate, so the Greeks and the Trojans held challenges of single combat outside the city walls. Achilles, the Greek champion, killed Hector, a Trojan prince. Achilles

■ *Achilles, champion of the Greeks.*

Write and Discuss

Today there is a sports injury known as *Achilles' heel*. What does it mean?

stripped the armor from Hector and towed Hector's body behind his chariot. This was seen as a great insult, and the Trojans could be heard crying and cursing from the city walls.

Homer's *Iliad* ends with Hector's funeral. But the legend of the Trojan War continues. Achilles seemed unbeatable, but he had a weak point. His heel did not have an armor protection. Soon after Hector's death, a Trojan arrow hit Achilles in the heel and crippled him. While he lay wounded on the ground, a Trojan ran in and finished him off.

■ *Greece and the Aegean Islands.*

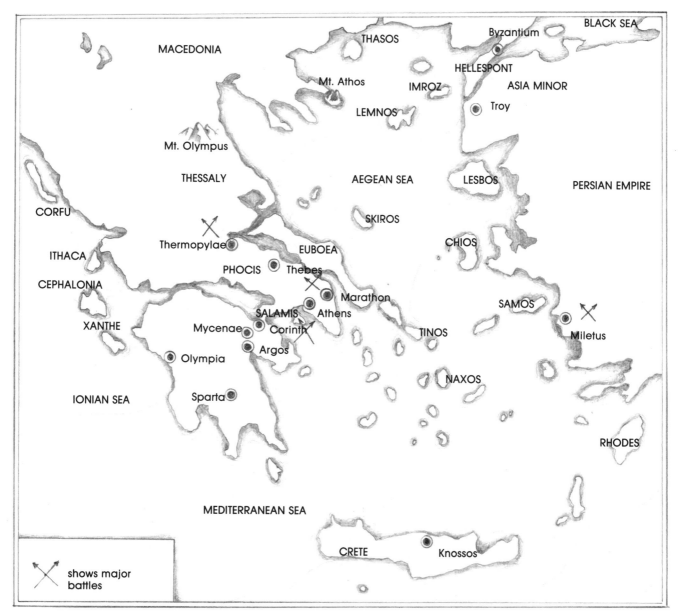

The Trojan Horse

After the death of Achilles, the Greeks thought of a way to end the siege and capture Troy. The Greeks built a huge wooden horse. Four Greeks hid inside it. The rest of the Greeks sailed away, leaving the wooden horse outside the walls of Troy.

The prophet Cassandra and the Trojan high priest warned the Trojans not to trust any gifts left by the Greeks. But the Trojans laughed. They saw the wooden horse as a trophy of victory and a sign of good luck.

■ *The wooden horse—a Greek gift.*

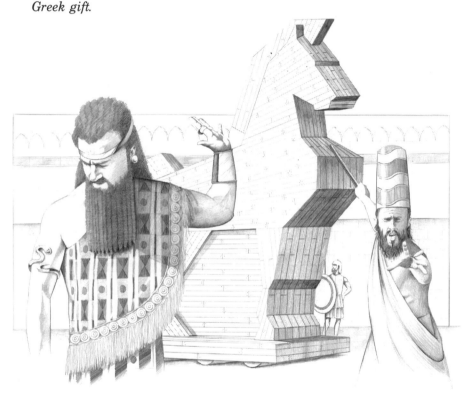

Activity

In a few lines, tell the story that is happening in the picture.

Write and Discuss

1. Why do you think there are two versions about Helen?

2. What was Achilles' weak point?

3. There is an old European proverb that says "Beware of Greeks bearing gifts." What would be the possible origin of this saying?

4. What was the purpose of the wooden horse?

5. Besides the *Iliad,* the poet Homer wrote a book called the *Odyssey.* This was the story of Odysseus, one of the Greek soldiers at the siege of Troy. In an encyclopedia or library book, find out more details about Odysseus.

The horse was too big to fit through the city gates, so the Trojans broke down a section of the city wall and pulled the huge wooden horse into the city square.

Late that night the Greeks inside the horse climbed down and ran to the beach. They lit a signal fire and the Greek ships sailed back in. That night, the Greeks broke into the city and killed nearly all the Trojans. They burned Troy to the ground and destroyed it. The Greeks then sailed home with Helen of Troy—"the face that launched a thousand ships."

The Legend Confirmed

Until the nineteenth century, people dated Greek history back until about 800 BC. This was all changed by several archaeologists who were able to push back the origins of Greece another 1,200 years.

The first archaeologists were Heinrich and Sophia Schliemann. Heinrich was a rich German businessman who went to the United States as a trader. He read Homer's *Iliad* and announced that he was going to use it as a guide to find the lost city of Troy. People told him that the *Iliad* was a fairy tale and it was madness to believe the story. But Schliemann suspected that the legend of Troy was based on the foundation of fact.

In 1873, the Schliemanns discovered the city walls of Troy in what is now Turkey. They found not one city but the ruins of nine other cities! After each city was knocked down, the next people built a new city on top of the ruins. The Schliemanns found a layer of ash that they guessed was the city burned down by the Greeks. They then found what they thought was the hidden treasure of King Priam of Troy.

Scholars no longer laughed at the dreamer Schliemann. What about the Greek invaders from Mycenae? Could the Schliemanns find King Agamemnon's palace at Mycenae?

The Schliemanns went to Mycenae on the mainland of Greece. Once again they discovered a treasure of graves, weapons, jewels, and ornaments at the royal tombs of Mycenae. They proved that there was an early Greek civilization 1,200 years before the later Greeks that were known about already. At Mycenae, the Schliemanns also found traces of pottery from Crete, an island of the Mediterranean. Heinrich died before he was able to dig up another civilization in Crete.

■ *Heinrich Schliemann at work.*

Activity

Heinrich and Sophia Schliemann were famous archaeologists. Other famous archaeologists were:

(a) Sir Flinders Petrie
(b) Sir Arthur Evans
(c) James Henry Breasted
(d) Dame Kathleen Kenyon

Using an encyclopedia, write short notes on the work of one of these archaeologists.

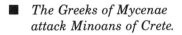

The Greeks of Mycenae attack Minoans of Crete.

Write and Discuss

1. When did the event pictured here occur?

2. The Greeks are face-to-face with a Minoan in the palace at _____.

3. What possible reasons were there for the Greeks to destroy the Minoan palace in Crete?

In 1900, Sir Arthur Evans from Britain found the palace of Knossos in Crete. The palace dated from about 2000 BC, but the Minoan civilization of Crete started about 4000 BC. The Minoans were great traders and their ships reached the mainland of Greece. In 1400 BC the Mycenaean Greeks attacked Crete and destroyed the palace at Knossos. The Mycenaean king tried to set up a new kingdom but was forced to leave the island because of attacks by Cretan rebels.

Further digging on mainland Greece by Sir Arthur Evans showed that the Mycenaean civilization ended by destruction from northern invaders around the year 1200 BC.

🪨 Rewriting the Dates

The work of the Schliemanns and Evans made it possible to fill in the early gaps in Greek history. It goes back much farther than previously thought. This is the new time line that we can trace back.

The Revised Greek Time Line

4500 BC	Neolithic people on Greek peninsula
3000–2200 BC	Bronze Age peoples arrive in Greece and Crete
1600 BC	Mycenaean kingdom established by Greeks from the north
1600–1400 BC	Growth of powerful Mycenaean kingdom with trading ships to Crete and Asia Minor
1450 BC	Destruction of Minoan Palace at Crete by Greeks of Mycenae
1230 BC	Troy destroyed by Greeks of Mycenae
1200 BC	Destruction of palaces of Mycenae in Greece
1200 BC	A new wave of Dorian Greeks from the north. These Dorian Greeks were the probable destroyers of Mycenae.
1100–900 BC	The New Iron Age takes over in Greece with new iron weapons and tools.
———	Previous cutoff line for Greek history until archaeologists Schliemann and Evans extended the story even farther back than 900 BC.
900 BC	Founding of the city-state of Sparta

🪨 Sparta—The Original Military State

In the twentieth century, there have been several attempts to set up a military state. In the 1930s, Nazi Germany, as well as Japan and Italy, tried to create countries where all the people were soldiers and fighters. They trained their young people to be fit and to obey orders without question. These young people were taught to be fierce, warlike, and without pity. Nazi Germany and Italy based their training on the ancient Spartans.

The Spartans were Dorian Greeks who conquered the original Greeks in their area of southern Greece. The Spartans used these defeated Greeks as their farmers. These semi-slaves were called *helots*. The Spartans spent their whole lives training as soldiers. They needed to be on guard because the helots outnumbered the Spartans by 10 to 1 and the Spartans needed to stop any rebellion.

The Spartan Life

The whole purpose of a Spartan's life was to be a soldier. Girls did not become soldiers but their training was very hard, too. They were expected to be strong and to have a soldier's outlook. A famous saying of a Spartan mother to her solider-son shows their idea about bravery: "Son, I want you to come home from the battle either carrying your shield or being carried dead on your shield. If you throw your spear and shield away in the battle, I do not want to see you dead or alive."

All girls had to perform gymnastics. When they grew up, they managed their own households, ran their own businesses, and were expected to have many Spartan babies (preferably boys). When a Spartan was born, the baby was presented to the elders, who examined the child for any deformities or defects. Imperfect children were thrown down a cliff at Taygetus.

At the age of seven the male children began their military training. They left home to live in an army barracks. Here they were taught two things—community living and discipline. Until he was 30 years old the Spartan man had to sleep in the barracks and have meals with his fellow soldiers. From 30 to 60 years of age the Spartan soldier could live at home but must have meals with his fellow soldiers at least once a day.

Discipline and hard living were encouraged. Each Spartan male had to spend a year living on his own in the wilderness. As apprentice soldiers, the Spartan men were deliberately starved so that they learned how to steal food. If they were caught, they were beaten—not for stealing but for being caught.

At their graduation ceremony, the young soldiers had to steal cheeses from a temple and run through a crowd of other soldiers. As they "ran the gauntlet," they were clubbed and beaten. Some even died from the ordeal. The survivors were accepted into the Spartan army.

The Spartans had no navy and no cavalry. They depended on their army as the power of the people. This army kept the helot slave population in control. Every year the Spartan army attacked the helots for practice. The Spartan army was used to expand the power of Sparta and conquer its neighbors.

Activity

A Spartan king named Archidamus proudly said this about his people: Our Spartan lives are worked out for us; we know where we are going and because we are sure we are brave in battle and defend our honor. Unlike other peoples we have self-control over ourselves. We are not highly educated but that's good too because we do not question our laws and customs. We just obey them.

Discuss and write down your opinion of living in Sparta as a military state. In your answer you might like to consider the following questions:

1. Would a Spartan life be boring or exciting?

2. Why was King Archidamus proud of the Spartans?

3. What were the main strengths and weaknesses of Spartan training?

4. Would you prefer your own way of life or the Spartan way of life?

The Spartan ideal is very attractive to some people. They admire the Spartans' hardness and bravery. Even today we show admiration for people by saying, "He lived a Spartan life of plain food and plain living!"

■ *Spartan girls had to learn dance and athletics.*

Write and Discuss

1. Why did the Spartans run the gauntlet? What purpose did this trial serve?

2. What kinds of events in modern life are like running a gauntlet? Do they serve the same purpose as the Spartan trial? Explain.

3. Do you think these kinds of trials make sense? Why?

■ *"Running the gauntlet"—Spartan style.*

Athens—A Greek City-State

Athens was the great rival of Sparta. They fought a long war against one another and were always jealous of each other. Like Sparta, Athens was a city-state. This meant that it was not a large country. Athens was a city of about 20,000 people. The farms around the city belonged to Athens, too.

This was the pattern of Greece. It was not one united country. Instead, there were many separate city-states like Athens, Corinth, Thebes, and Sparta.

Athens was a typical Greek city-state. Athens was very different from Sparta. In Sparta the state was more important than each person. In Athens each person was the most important unit of the state. Pericles, an Athenian leader, proudly said:

> Other States [like Sparta] like people who keep quiet and do not involve themselves in what happens around them. We Athenians regard such quiet, obedient people as worse than useless. Athens expects all people to take an active part in how the state is run.

Athens was one of the first states to introduce **democracy** as a form of government. *Demos* means "people."

Activity

The Parthenon was a famous temple to the Greek goddess Athena. Compare this drawing of the Parthenon with a photograph of the ruins today. We can still recognize that it is the Parthenon but it now has been partly destroyed. There are four reasons:

1. The great age of the temple.

2. The earthquakes in Athens over the years.

3. The explosion of Turkish gunpowder inside the temple in 1687.

4. The pollution from car exhaust in Athens.

See what further information you can discover about any one of these facts.

Athens went through several stages of government. To begin with, Athens had kings as rulers. The kings were the leaders of all the religious festivals. The king had a council of rich landowners. They elected three *archons,* or judges, every year.

These landowners became very rich and took over from the king. Athens was now ruled by a small, rich group called the *oligarchs.* They believed that the people with the most wealth should run the country. This new **oligarchy** was superior to the *ecclesia,* or council of citizens. The smaller farmers fell into debt during bad years and lost their farms to the new rulers.

The Athenian people rebelled against this system and a new type of leader called a *tyrant* now ruled Athens for the poor people rather than the rich people. In 508 BC, one of these tyrants, Cleisthenes, changed the voting rules so that even the poor citizens had an equal say in the government. A council of 500 members met in Athens to decide matters of government.

Athens now had a democratic government. Cleisthenes introduced a new idea to prevent one person from becoming too powerful and acting against the wishes of the people.

■ *The Parthenon at Athens.*

Every year all the citizens (male only) met in Athens for a general assembly meeting of the whole council. They voted on who was the most unpopular person in Athens for that year. They scratched the name on a scrap piece of clay, called an **ostracon.** If one man got 6,000 votes, he was banned from Athens for 10 years. This idea was to stop any one person from becoming a dictator or not listening to the wishes of the people.

Activity

Look up the words *ostra-cize* and *ostracism* in a dictionary. How are they related to the Athenian ostracon?

What other English words can you discover that have Greek roots? What kinds of occupa-tions and activities seem to have a lot of words that came from Greek? What does this suggest about Ancient Greek society?

■ *Destroying the ostraca.*

The Olympic Games

In 1896, the first modern Olympic Games were held in Athens. Every four years the Olympic Games are held in a different city of the world. Even countries who do not like one another forget their arguments and compete at the Olympic games. Athens has applied to have the 1996 Olympic Games again on the one hundredth anniversary of the first modern Olympic Games.

The Olympic Games were first held in Greece in ancient times. The first games were held in 776 BC and then every four years until AD 394. The original games were not only a sporting event but also a religious festival.

They were called the Olympic Games because the games were originally held at Olympia. Olympia was a holy place belonging to the god Zeus, who was the king of the Greek gods. Every four years messengers were sent out from Olympia to all the Greek city-states. These messengers wore crowns of olive branches and were known as the heralds of peace. They announced the "truce of sport," which meant that even Greek city-states that were at war had to stop to attend the games.

Competitors and spectators from all over Greece went to Olympia. Olympia was not a town, so they camped there for at least one week. All the competitors had to prove to the judges that they were Greek. Everyone joined in to offer a sacrifice to the gods. Then there was a feast and the athletes made their oath. They swore that they had trained for the games and that they would not cheat.

There were horse races and chariot races between the different city-states. There were running races at the stadium. The stadium had a straight track of 200 meters made up of sand with eight lanes. (There was no circular track for longer races.) The most popular event was the pentathlon. This was a five-event contest in which the athletes had to perform well at different types of sports. These events were:

- *Long jump.* There was a sand jumping pit with marker pegs just like modern long jumps. The jumpers carried a 2-kilogram weight in each hand and, when they jumped, they swung their arms forward to give themselves greater forward thrust.

- *Discus throw.* At the funeral games at Troy, the Greek athletes threw a lump of iron. By 300 BC the athletes were throwing an iron plate weighing about 3 kilograms.

- *Javelin throw.* The javelin was a 2-meter-long wooden spear. It had a leather strap into which the thrower slipped two fingers. This added extra power to the throw.

- *Wrestling.* The object of this event was to throw your opponent to the ground. There was no time count. Tripping was allowed.

- *Boxing.* This was a cruel type of boxing with little covering over the fists. The boxers were not allowed to gouge eyes but most other punches were allowed.

Some Unusual Features of the Ancient Olympics

1. Chariot races were the most highly prized events. Kings as far away as the Greek colony of Syracuse in Sicily traveled to win the olive crown for this race.

2. For most of the ancient Olympic games, women were not only forbidden to take part in the games, they were not even allowed to watch the events. Only the priestesses of the holy Olympic temples could watch.

3. One of the races was for soldiers in full uniform and armor.

4. As well as sporting events, there were contests in plays, songs, and music playing. The Roman emperor Nero was later to be a winner of some of these events.

 *Boxing at ancient Olympia.*

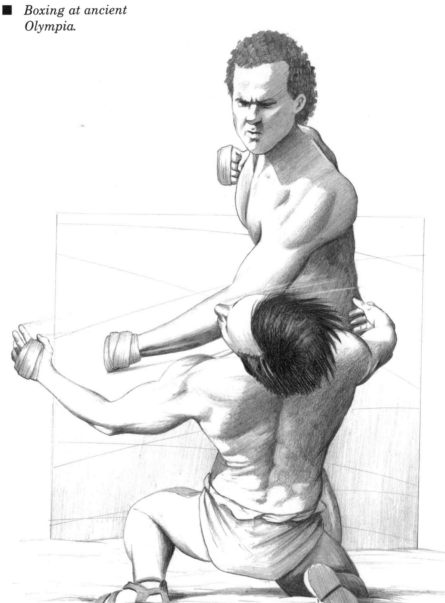

Write and Discuss

1. The modern Olympics have a pentathlon and a decathlon medal. What are the five events of the pentathlon and the 10 events of the decathlon?

2. Why was Ancient Greek boxing more cruel than modern boxing? Why is boxing banned in some countries today?

3. What are some other sports in the modern Olympic Games that were not found in the ancient Games?

5. There was no marathon race in the ancient Olympic Games. In 490 BC, the Athenian army faced an invading army of Persians in a plain called Marathon, about 40 kilometers or 25 miles from Athens. The Persian army wanted to overthrow Athens. After several days of fighting, some of the Persian army loaded on to ships, planning to sail to Athens and attack the city by sea. The Athenian army surrounded and defeated the remaining Persians. Then they marched to Athens before the Persian ships arrived. The Athenian victory kept Greece from becoming part of the Persian Empire.

According to legend, the Athenians sent their best runner, Pheidippides, to Athens to announce the Athenians' victory. He ran the full distance at full speed, delivered the message, and dropped dead. The modern marathon race is named in his honor.

The Persian Invasion

Greece was always ripe for invasion by a powerful neighbor. Greece was never a united country but a collection of separate city-states. These city-states were so jealous of each other that sometimes they would not help each other even when everyone was in danger from an outside power.

By 500 BC the Persian Empire of the Middle East was expanding westward. Greek settlers had set up states in the Aegean Sea. Lesbos, Chios, and Samos had thriving Greek colonies. Some Greeks had settled along the coast of Asia Minor, from Troy in the north to Miletus in the south.

The Persian king Darius demanded that these eastern Greek settlers accept his authority. The proud Greek cities and islands refused. The Persians collected a fleet of 600 Egyptian and Phoenician ships. The eastern Greeks collected 350 of their own. The states of Miletus, Chios, Lesbos, and Samos joined together to fight as one fleet. The usual method for naval battle up until then was to sail alongside and grapple with the enemy. The soldiers of the two ships fought it out and the winner gained a second ship.

The Greeks had developed a new, fast fighting ship called a **trireme.** The trireme had 170 rowers in three rows on each side. The extra line of rowers meant that the Greek ships were very fast. The new Greek trireme also had a pointed beak at the front below the waterline. The trireme would try to ram into the side of the enemy ship, then row backwards and watch the enemy sink. That was the theory, anyway. However, the Greek commander of one fleet had a

■ *A Greek trireme.*

new idea. The idea was to row straight at the front of the enemy ship. Using split-second timing, the Greek oarsmen would pull in their oars and their ship would brush the enemy ship, shaving all their oars off like matchsticks. The enemy ship would then be helpless in the water and could easily be rammed in the middle.

The trireme and these tactics were to make the Athenian fleet the best in the world later in the century. But in the battle near Miletus the Greek fleet failed. The Samians went over to the Persians and the Lesbos fleet sailed off in fright. The rest of the fleet from Chios and Miletus fought to the end but were destroyed by superior numbers.

In 490 BC the Persians set out with their invasion fleet for Athens. Their army of 25,000 soldiers and 1,000 horses attacked the island of Naxos, then sailed on to the island of Euboea where they landed to get ready for their attack on Athens.

The Persian army landed at Marathon and got ready to march to Athens. The Athenian army of 10,000 rushed northward to Marathon and had a smashing victory. The remainder of the Persian army was just able to get back on their ships and sail back home across the Aegean Sea.

The Persians Try Again

After the Persian king Darius died, his son Xerxes decided to see if he could capture the whole of Greece. Instead of sailing across the Aegean Sea, his huge army marched all the way from Asia Minor. Xerxes built a 12-kilometer (about 7.5 miles) bridge across the Hellespont so that his army could march from Asia to the European side. Xerxes had a fleet of over 600 ships that hugged the coast, level with the army as it marched. At Mount Athos the Persians dug a canal through the peninsula so that the fleet did not have to sail around the stormy cape.

As Xerxes advanced, he sent messengers ahead to demand surrender. Macedonia, Thessaly, and Thebes surrendered but Athens and Sparta refused. The Spartans quickly finished building a wall across the land north of Corinth. Themistocles, the Athenian leader, sent all the citizens of Athens to a nearby island and prepared the Athenian fleet near the island of Salamis.

The Spartans stayed behind their wall at Corinth but sent King Leonidas and 300 Spartans up the east coast as their gift to the Greek army. When the Spartans reached the narrow mountain pass at Thermopylae, they found only 1,000 Phocians there to help them. The Persian army had to break through this narrow pass if they were to advance farther south.

Persian spies went ahead and were surprised to see the Spartans combing their hair. The Spartans were preparing for death, as they knew they had no hope against the 40,000 Persians. King Leonidas sent the other Greek forces home with thanks and prepared to meet the Persians.

The Persians could not attack with all their force because of the narrow valley. For two days the Spartans held them back. Then a Greek traitor showed the Persians a mountain track around behind the Spartans. The Spartans were surrounded. For nearly all of the third day the Spartans fought on until the arrows of the enemy had reduced them to 50 men. The Spartans then retreated to a mound around their king and fought on until the last man was dead.

After the battle the Spartan bodies were collected and buried in a mass grave. A small hill was built on top as a memorial. Even today, on top of the hill there is a stone monument with this message written in Greek:

> Go stranger and tell the Spartans that here we lie, still obedient to your orders.

The Persian army swarmed southward and destroyed Athens. Then the Athenian fleet tried the same trick as the Spartan army at Thermopylae. In open sea the Persian fleet would outnumber the Greek fleet. Therefore, the Greek fleet pulled back into the narrow waters beside the island of Salamis. In the narrow strait, the Persian fleet was restricted, and the Greek fleet was able to win the battle.

Xerxes left a part of his army in Greece but took most of his army back up the coast. When he retreated to the Hellespont, he found that his bridge had been destroyed by storms. Xerxes' fleet ferried the Persian survivors back to Asia Minor. The Persian threat had been finally defeated.

Write and Discuss

"King Leonidas and his 300 men were true to the Spartan standards at Thermopylae." In what ways did they show themselves to be true Spartans?

Activity
Trace a map of Greece
and the Aegean Sea
area. Use the text and the
text map as a guide.
Draw in the route of the
Persian invasion of Xerxes
in 480 BC. On your map
write in all the places and
islands that were men-
tioned in the text.

■ *The Spartans' last stand
at Thermopylae.*

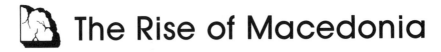 The Rise of Macedonia

The next hundred years for Greece was a period of war and confusion.
The Greeks had defeated the Persians and were now stronger than
ever. But instead of joining together, the Greek city-states began to
fight with one another. Athens became the strongest state but then
a bitter war broke out with Sparta. Sparta won the war and took over
most of Greece. Then Thebes challenged Sparta and Thebes became
the strongest state. A hundred years of wars began to wear out the
southern Greeks. They had spent so much in people and money to beat
one another that now they were no longer the wealthy leading states
of Greece.

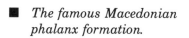

■ *The famous Macedonian phalanx formation.*

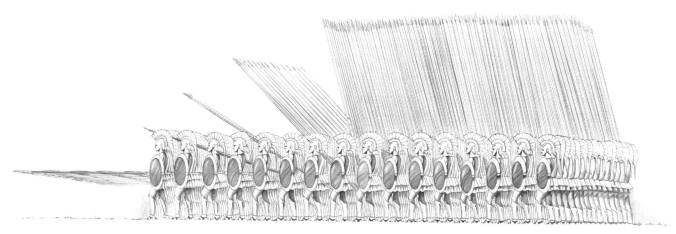

Write and Discuss

1. How many rows of spears poked out from the front line of soldiers?

2. Why are the other rows of spears half ready to come down level?

3. What protection could the spears in the air give the back rows of the soldiers?

4. It was said that the Macedonian phalanx had a bulldozer effect on the enemy. Why would this be so?

5. A spearman in the third row who got wounded by an arrow would not have a chance to get first aid. Why would this be so?

The new state that began to grow in power was the state of Macedonia. In 359 BC, Philip became the new king. He was a great military leader. The Macedonian army was famous for its wild cavalry that charged their enemies with great dash. Philip had been a prisoner of the Thebans and had watched their foot soldiers practicing their famous phalanx formation. Soon he organized his Macedonian army in the same way.

Philip began a 20-year fight to become the ruler of all of Greece. By 338 BC, he had defeated the Athenians and had become the ruler of the whole of Greece. Philip was not a hard victor. He called all the Greek states to Corinth where they met to discuss an invasion of Persia. But it was not to be. In 336 BC, Philip was stabbed to death as he walked in procession in a public celebration. He was buried with great sorrow in an underground tomb. In 1974 archaeologists found his tomb with some remarkable objects inside it.

■ *A battle scene from Philip the Great's tomb.*

Alexander the Great

After Philip's death, the new king of Macedonia was Alexander, a 20-year-old who was already an experienced army commander. Alexander decided to carry out his father's wish—to defeat the Persian king and be the ruler of the whole of Asia. For 13 years Alexander led his Greek army through Asia and Egypt. Not once did they return home. The soldiers followed him all the way to the Indus River, where they finally refused to go any farther.

Alexander died at the early age of 33, a leader whose army followed him to the ends of the known world. This book is too small to tell his whole story. The map shows the 13-year journey of Alexander and his army. One of Alexander's generals was Ptolemy, who later became the king of Egypt. Ptolemy wrote the story of Alexander's journey. The rest of this section about Alexander the Great is based on Ptolemy's history.

■ *The expedition of Alexander and his Greek army.*

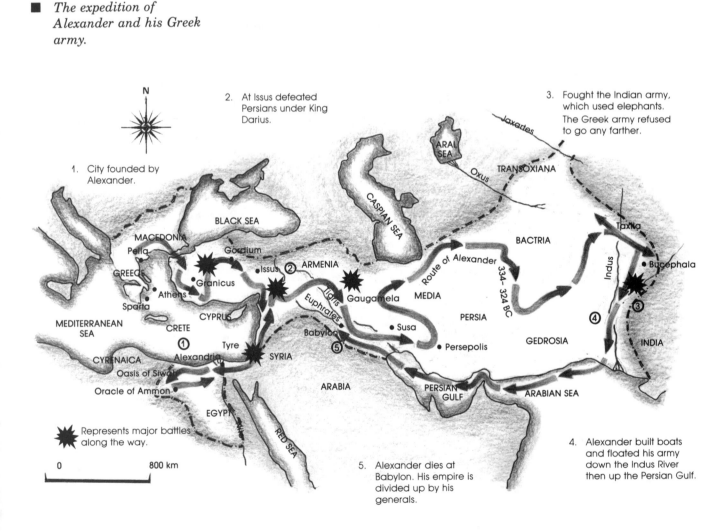

2. At Issus defeated Persians under King Darius.

3. Fought the Indian army, which used elephants. The Greek army refused to go any farther.

1. City founded by Alexander.

Represents major battles along the way.

0   800 km

5. Alexander dies at Babylon. His empire is divided up by his generals.

4. Alexander built boats and floated his army down the Indus River then up the Persian Gulf.

Solving the Problem

The army wintered in the ancient city of Gordium. They were waiting for new troops from Greece. They were waiting for the spring crops to grow so they could move on to Issus. There in the old palace was an old chariot. Around its yoke was a knot of bark tied round and round in a thick knot. The philosophers said that whoever could undo the knot would rule the whole of Asia. Alexander tried and tried but could not undo the knot. He was not defeated. He drew his sword and cut the knot in half. He was destined to rule Asia.

The Fall of Tyre

The Persian city of Tyre was an island with half a mile of sea on the shore side. Alexander began building a log-and-earth causeway across the water so that his siege machines could attack the walls. The water was so deep, however, that it took three months to get within catapult range. The defenders of Tyre fought the Greeks off with arrow catapults and fire ships that burned down the wooden bridges from the causeway. The Greek fleet surrounded the city of Tyre, and after six months the Tyre fleet was destroyed in an attempt to break the siege. Alexander's siege ships with battering rams and towers finally broke through. Alexander personally led the attack and was wounded with an arrow.

■ *Alexander's cavalry defeated the Persian army at Tyre.*

Write and Discuss

1. Why did Alexander's men refuse to go any farther?

2. How did he feel about turning back?

3. How did they face the problem of the rains and rising rivers that blocked their path?

No Farther

At the River Beas (which fed into the Indus River) the men would go no farther. They had marched 11,000 miles in seven years. The monsoon was now upon them. They tried to sleep in hammocks to avoid the deadly snakes. Alexander sulked in his tent. He dreamt of new kingdoms across the river and across the next river.

However, the army could not go on, they would not go on. Their weapons were rusty and their uniforms were rotting. They had faced the elephants; they had done what no one had done.

The army could not ford all the rivers in flood but this did not stop them. Instead, they would sail the 1,200 kilometers (over 700 miles) to the sea. Alexander's men set about building 800 flat-bottom boats to sail down the Indus River. Within two months 120,000 men, stores, and 15,000 horses were on their homeward journey.

But where was home now? They were a lifetime away from their Greeks homes.

■ *Alexander's army faces the enemy's elephants in northern India.*

The Greeks could not handle the elephants with their weapons. Instead the foot soldiers allowed the elephants to break through their lines. The soldiers dodged sideways and then reformed their line to face the enemy soldiers. It was not easy to turn the charging elephants and attack the Greeks from behind. Some of the Greeks hacked the hamstrings of the elephants' back legs and crippled them.

Alexander's Death

Worn down with wounds, worn out with fever, Alexander at last reached Babylon. Alexander sent his general, Nearchus, against Arabia. That night a party was held and Alexander drank deeply.

All at once he shouted out and fell back. He was carried to his room where the fever grew upon him. For eight days he lingered on. On the eighth day the army rioted. "He is dead," they shouted. They would not be quiet but threatened to kill their officers and break into the palace unless Alexander was shown to them.

All that day his men streamed past his bed. Alexander could not speak by this time but rolled his eyes and nodded to his men. That night his generals crowded around to say goodbye. "Who will lead us? Who will be the king?" Alexander whispered, "To the best, to the best."

The Downfall of Greece

After the death of Alexander, the huge empire that he had captured broke up. His generals divided it into kingdoms. One general took Babylon and Asia Minor. Ptolemy began a new dynasty of pharaohs in Egypt. Alexander's half brother was named king of Macedonia and Greece, but two generals kept control of Macedonia and the rest of Greece. For the next 100 years Macedonia was the leader of Greece, although the Spartans and Athenians tried several times to shake off Macedonian control.

Greece eventually came under the control of the Roman Empire. It happened in this way. Carthage and Rome were at war to decide which country was to control the Mediterranean Sea. In 217 BC, Philip V of Macedonia made a treaty with Hannibal of Carthage so that Hannibal had the help of some Greek island colonies. In 200 BC, the Romans declared war on Macedonia. The southern Greeks went over to the Roman side and the Macedonians were defeated.

This was the end of Macedonian control of Greeks. But it was not the end of Roman control. The Romans extended their control so that by 150 BC the whole of Greece had become a Roman colony.

A final incident gives us some idea of what happened to Greece under the rule of the Roman "barbarians." The Roman consul Mummius ransacked Corinth and sent all the priceless Greek statues as booty back to Rome. He warned the captains that any statues damaged on the voyage home would have to be replaced by new ones! So much for Greek antiques.

The Legacy of Greek Architecture

Roman builders copied most of their architecture from the Greeks. In particular they copied their public buildings from the Greek model. Such buildings as temples, senate chambers, and baths were based on Greek architecture.

A common feature of Greek architecture was the use of columns. The columns were the main walls of the buildings, carrying the load of the roof. Look at the illustration of the front of a typical temple. Three styles of columns developed in three different areas of Greece. The three styles were **Doric, Ionic,** and **Corinthian**.

The Greeks also decorated walls with paintings. On most temples the **pediment,** or top section above the columns, often had scenes carved into the marble. Often they were of victories or battles.

Corinthian   Doric   Ionic

■ *The three main styles of Greek columns in buildings.*

Activity

Modern courthouses, houses of parliament, museums and art galleries, war memorials, and fronts of churches sometimes copy the Greek architectural style. Obtain a photograph or sketch of a building you know with such columns.

1. What styles do the columns follow?

2. Are the columns made of one piece of stone or of several pieces joined together?

■ *The basic Greek model for a temple or public building.*

Activity

Ask your teacher to photocopy the black-and-white wall painting from the Minoan Palace at Crete. Color in the painting as you interpret it. Perhaps the monkey is eating a flower or fruit. What do the wavy lines suggest to you?

The oldest painting that we have is the reconstruction of a wall painting in the palace at Knossos in Crete. Sir Arthur Evans found fragments of this wall painting and was able to build up the missing parts.

The painting is mysterious. It seems that the birds are rock doves that nest in rocks. There is a monkey eating what appears to be an egg and another monkey searching for eggs in a papyrus bush. There

■ *A reconstruction of a wall painting in the Palace of Knossos in Crete.*

seem to be round eggs resting along the base line of the painting. The monkey eating the egg has an orange muzzle, which seems to indicate egg yolk. The wavy lines through the painting were black and blue.

Greek Domestic Art

The Ancient Greeks were masters at clay pottery. They made cups, bowls, jars, and jugs. Greek artisans also made beautiful vases on which they painted people and scenes.

The vase in the illustration shows two Greek boxers and two Greek wrestlers. Usually Greek artists drew people true-to-life, but in this case the artist emphasized the hips and thighs of the athletes to impress us with their strength. Many of these delicate vases were preserved because they were carefully buried in tombs.

You will notice that there are also painted designs around the vase. These colored bands were often painted on simpler cups and jugs. Many of these designs became traditional in Europe. Some are still used today.

■ *A fine example of a Greek vase found in a Greek tomb.*

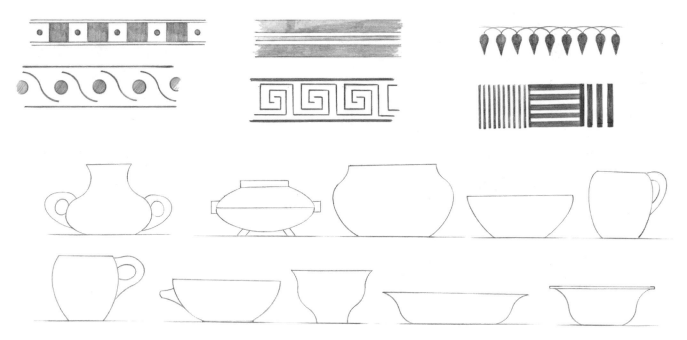

■ *Types of Greek pottery and common designs for decorating the edges of the pottery.*

Activity

Look at the series of band decoration designs from Greek pottery. Pictured also are a series of Ancient Greek cups, bowls, vases, and jugs. Choose four different kinds of clay vessels and explain how each might have been used.

Redraw the Greek clay vessels and choose several band designs to decorate the bowls. Red and black were common design colors.

The Story Continues

The Romans ruled Greece until AD 395. When Constantinople became the eastern capital of the Roman Empire, Greece was ruled from this eastern capital rather than from Rome.

In the 400s, Greece was raided by the Vandals, the Goths, and the Huns. The Eastern Roman Empire survived these attacks. The Greeks adopted the customs of the Eastern Church of Byzantium (Constantinople) rather than follow the church customs of Rome. That is why even today the Greek Orthodox Churches are greatly different from the Catholic or Protestant Churches of Western Europe.

In 1453, the Muslim Turks took over the whole of Eastern Europe, including Greece. Greece was ruled by Turkey for nearly 400 years.

Finally, in 1829, Greece won a war of independence from Turkey and became a free country again. During the nineteenth and twentieth centuries Greece invited kings from Germany and Denmark to rule the country. This was not a great success. Greece is now a united republic with a democratic form of government.

After World War II (1939–1945), many Greeks left Greece to settle in the United States, South America, and Australia.

Chapter Five

Rome

A Great Empire

Kings of Rome
(753–509 BC)

Rome was founded in approximately 753 BC. The legend is that Romulus and Remus, two brothers, built the first city walls. The Roman people were ruled by the kings of the main people in central Italy. These were the Etruscans. In 509 BC, the Roman people threw off the rule of these kings. The last king of the Romans was named Tarquinius Superbus. The Romans hated this rule by kings. They swore never to bow to any king in the future.

Once they were free of kings, the Roman people of the city began to spread their power over the whole of Italy.

The Republic of Rome
(509–27 BC)

The Roman people decided on a new form of government called a **republic**. The word comes from two Latin words, *res publica*, which

■ *Roman senators.*

translates as "the affairs of the people." A senate of 300 members was elected to run the country. These senators were elected for life. It was their job to make laws, elect officials, and be the judges in important matters. The senate elected two **consuls** each year to run the country from day to day. In time of war, one of these consuls took command of the army while the other stayed at home in Rome.

The Republic of Rome was not a democracy where everyone has an equal say. Roman society was divided into two main groups. The **patricians** were the wealthy people. The **plebeians** were the poor people. The senators were all wealthy landowners. In the beginning only the wealthy landowners had a vote.

The plebeians were given some say in the senate. Two senators were elected as **tribunes**. They looked after the rights of the plebeians. The tribunes could veto (forbid) any law they thought would harm the plebeians. The number of tribunes was later increased to 10.

As the years went by, the Roman Republic developed a system of officials to run a country that was becoming more and more important. As the Republic of Rome grew, the number of officials grew. By the time of the end of the Roman Republic there were government officials for every purpose. There was a Roman public service as large as that in any modern country like the United States. The officials were appointed by the senate.

■ *Roman senators debating
in the senate. Each senator
wore an official toga, or
cloak, which was a sign of
his special importance.*

Public Servants of the Roman Republic

Consul.   Two of these were appointed each year. They were prime
ministers for the year. Each consul had equal power. The consuls always had 12 *lictors* with them. These were judges who
carried sticks and axes over their shoulders. These were to
show that the consul had the power of punishment and execution. In times of emergency, a consul could be elected as a dictator for six months.

Pro-Consuls.   These were retired consuls who were sent out as
governors of cities and colonies of Rome. Pontius Pilate of Jerusalem was a pro-consul in Jesus Christ's time.

Praetors.   There were eight praetors appointed. They were judges
who traveled around the republic judging serious cases, such as
treason or stealing by one of the generals.

Tribunes.   Two senators were elected as tribunes. They looked
after the rights of the plebeians. No tribune could be arrested
or punished while doing his job. Later, tribunes were elected as
political officers in the army.

Activity

Review the brief descrip-
tions of jobs in Roman
public service. Take the
part of one of these officials and write a short
speech to be read out
loud to the senate (your
class). The speech will be
about an urgent matter
that you wish to make
known to the senate. The
senate must decide what
to do in each case.

Some possible begin-
nings for speeches are
listed here. Use an ency-
clopedia, history book,
and your imagination to
write your speech.

Consul: "Senators of
Rome, I have to report to
you about a disaster that
has happened to the
eighth legion in Spain."

Pro-Consul: "Senators, this
is my annual report to you
about our colony in
Britain."

Praetor: "Senators, I wish
to inform you about the
bribery of Varrus, our governor in Sicily."

Tribune: "Senators, the
unfair prices for food will
have to stop."

Quaestor: "This year our
taxes from Egypt are
down because of the fail-
ure of the Nile to flood as
it usually does."

Pontifex: "Last night a sac-
rilege happened at the
Temple of Jupiter. Some
young hooligans . . ."

Censor: "The small number of births over the last year has serious consequences for our future Roman army."

Quaestor. The quaestor was a judge who controlled the money. He was like the treasurer today. Sub-quaestors (about 20) would be involved in tax collecting and payment of wages to the army.

Pontifex. He was a priest in charge of sacrifices and ceremonies. He could be elected from the army as was Julius Caesar for one year. It was a stepping stone to higher office. The chief priest was pontifex maximus. There might be 15 pontifices under his control. In Christian times, the pope took the same title—pontifex maximus.

Censor. Two censors were elected at a time. They were in charge of taking the census each year and running the elections. They were like the modern Census Bureau. The censor was also in charge of looking out for public morals.

The Roman Empire (27 BC–AD 476)

One of Rome's greatest generals, Julius Caesar, was responsible for the extension of the Roman Empire far beyond the old boundaries of Rome. Julius Caesar was one of a group of Roman generals who wanted to show their power and ability. These generals were Pompey, Crassus, and Caesar. They divided the empire between them and each ruled a section. But then a series of civil wars began between them. By 48 BC, Julius Caesar had defeated the other two and had become dictator of Rome.

A group of senators plotted to kill him. They were afraid that he would be crowned king and would finish the republic and the senate. On March 15, 44 BC, Caesar was stabbed to death in the senate. Many senators stabbed him so that no single person would be blamed later. They told the angry Roman people that they had killed Caesar because they loved Rome more than him, but most people knew that fear and jealousy were behind the murder.

The Republic did not last long after this. In 30 BC, Caesar's nephew, Octavius, became the most powerful general. Octavius became the first Roman emperor. This meant single rule by one man. Octavius carefully avoided the hated word *king*.

The senate now became a rubber stamp to approve what the emperor did. This new line of emperors had a huge army of up to 25 legions behind them. They had become too powerful for the senate to control as in the past. The emperor with his army was now able to make quick decisions and act when there was an urgent need.

As the years progressed, this empire became larger. The map shows the Roman Empire in AD 190.

This empire depended very much on the quality of the emperor. When there was an able emperor, the empire prospered. If there was an unstable or poor emperor, then the empire suffered. Sometimes an emperor became emperor because he had the biggest army when the old emperor died. This system of empire lasted until AD 476. After that date, invaders from the north captured parts of the empire. At several times, Rome itself was overrun by these barbarians. The Roman Empire was no longer strong enough to hold together as one unit.

Famous Roman Emperors

Between the years 27 BC and AD 476, Rome was an empire. Instead of being a republic with senators as rulers, an emperor ruled the empire. The empire stretched from Scotland to North Africa, from Spain to Syria. Most of Europe was ruled from Rome. During this time there were some remarkable emperors. These are the stories of a few of them.

■ *Nero, emperor of Rome. This illustration is copied from a statue of Nero.*

Nero

Nero ruled Rome from AD 54 to 68. He came to the throne at the age of 16. He was under the control of his mother, Agrippina. In AD 59 when Agrippina tried to take over, her son Nero had her killed. He murdered his own wife, Octavia, because he thought she was plotting against him.

Nero went to Greece, which was then a Roman colony, and ran in the Olympic Games and sang at music festivals. He won 200 gold medals himself (a world record!). Some think he may have cheated in a few races and singing contests.

When he returned to Rome he had a grand plan to rebuild Rome. Half of Rome mysteriously burned down, and many were suspicious of Nero, who had new plans already drawn. Nero blamed the new Christians and thousands of them were burned alive on posts with tar along the main road out of Rome.

Nero neglected the army, and a revolt of the army broke out in France. The Roman general Galba came to Rome as the new emperor. Nero committed suicide rather than be killed by his own army.

Vespasian

Vespasian took over government soon after the death of Nero. He ruled from AD 69 to 79. Vespasian and his son Titus put down the rebellion of the Jews and gained the final defeat of the Jews at Masada in AD 73. Many of these Jewish rebels were brought to Rome to work on Vespasian's famous building, the Colosseum.

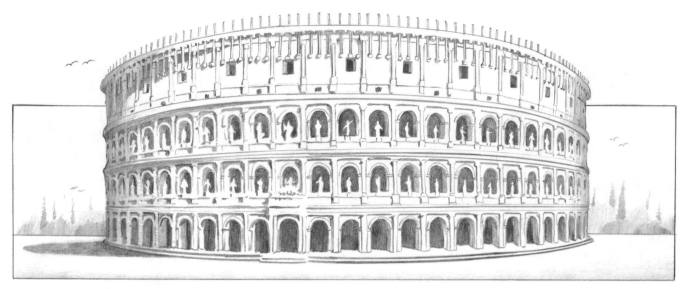

■ *The Colosseum of Rome—
before some of it was
knocked down to be reused
as building blocks.*

Activities

1. Find a photograph of the Colosseum. What parts of the building are now missing?

2. The 80 doorways could empty the stadium in five minutes. The Latin word for these doorway exits was *vomitaria*. What English word have we borrowed from this word? What does the word mean in English?

The Colosseum was a huge sports stadium that could seat 60,000 spectators. The whole stadium could be cleared in five minutes with 80 doorways leading out to the road. The Colosseum got its name from the colossal statue of Apollo outside the stadium. The people began to refer to the stadium as the *colossus*.

The colosseum is a remarkable building because of the use of concrete in the floors and the roofs. Built to last, the Colosseum did not fall down of age or natural causes. Over the centuries, Romans tore down the stone blocks to make their own houses. The ruins are now protected from such vandalism.

Vespasian was a capable emperor who chose his governors wisely. He reformed the tax system and made Rome rich again. On his deathbed he is supposed to have said, "It looks like I am going to turn into a god very soon."

Hadrian

Hadrian was truly an emperor. He ruled from AD 117 to 138 and spent more than 10 years traveling around the empire inspecting the army and the colonies. Hadrian pulled back his armies from further extension of the empire. To protect the empire he had, he built forts along the Danube and Rhine rivers to protect his boundaries. In Roman Britain, he built his famous wall across the island. This was to protect Britain from raids across the Scottish border. This wall still exists today. It was a remarkable building achievement. It was 130 kilometers (about 80 miles) long with 80 small castles along it.

■ *Roman soldiers watch out from Hadrian's Wall.*

Write and Discuss

1. Who were the soldiers watching out for?

2. Why did the wall have 80 little castles along it?

3. How do you think the soldiers guarded the wall at night to make sure no enemies crept over?

Hadrian was born in Spain and was regarded as an outsider by the Roman senate. When he first made a speech in the senate, they laughed at his accent. He saw his job as traveling around the empire, not sitting in Rome. He is remembered as an able emperor who did his best to keep the empire together.

Didius Julianus

By the end of the second century, the Roman Empire was becoming weaker. The barbarians from Eastern Europe were continually attacking across the Danube and Rhine rivers. These attacks were very expensive to the Roman army. Another problem was that the job of emperor did not always go to the son of the dead emperor. When an emperor died, there was often a bitter civil war to see who would be the next emperor. In addition, the bodyguards of the emperor were becoming a constant threat to the emperor. The **praetorian guard**, which was supposed to guard the emperor, instead began the practice of killing the emperor and replacing him with their own emperor.

In AD 193, a new emperor, Pertinax, was elected. He announced that he intended to cut down the wild spending of the army. The praetorian guard rose up and killed Pertinax. They placed the emperor's head on a spear and marched to the center of Rome. Here they announced that they would sell the job of emperor to the highest bidder. Several senators bid for the honor. An old senator, Didius Julianus, promised each praetorian guard an amount of money that was a fortune in those days. He was declared the winner by the praetorian guard, who marched him off to the senate and forced them to vote him in.

When word of this event reached the armies of the colonies, four generals announced that they would march on Rome to avenge the insult to Roman honor (and make themselves the emperor).

One of these generals, Septimius Severus, reached Rome first. He was able to bluff the praetorian guard with his own army from Germany. Didius Julianus was arrested and beheaded. Septimius Severus later defeated the other generals who were marching on Rome to claim the emperor's title.

The short reign of Didius Julianus lasted only 60 days. He was not an important emperor but his reign shows how the once-great Rome had sunk into disorder. Generals no longer wanted to become emperors to help Rome. They used the job of emperor for their own glory.

Constantine

Constantine ruled the Roman Empire from AD 307 to 337. At times he shared the rule of the empire with others. In 312 Constantine overthrew Maxentius who had ruled with him for several years. In 324 he also overthrew Licinius, who had shared the empire with him for over 10 years.

Until Constantine, Christians had been persecuted and executed by Roman emperors. Christians were regarded as different and with no real loyalty to Rome. Constantine changed all that. He gave his official support to Christianity. Instead of Christians being the hated

■ *A member of the emperor's praetorian bodyguard.*

Activities

1. Only a few Roman emperors have been mentioned here. There were many other interesting (and sometimes crazy) emperors. Find some details about the following emperors:

   ■ Caligula (AD 37–41, nicknamed "little boot")

   ■ Trajan (AD 98–117)

   ■ Marcus Aurelius (AD 161–180)

   ■ Diocletian (AD 284–305)

2. The Colosseum is only one of the huge buildings that the Romans built. Ruins of aqueducts, city walls, and bridges still remain as evidence of the great ability they had. See if you can find pictures and information about some of these.

3. Of the five emperors you have read about in this book, which did the most for Rome? Write down your reasons. Which one seems to you to be the worst emperor or the one who didn't care about Rome as much as himself? Write down your reason for your choice.

4. One of the problems of the new emperor was that he did not inherit the title of emperor, that is, he was often not a relation of the previous emperor. Instead, the new emperor was usually a strong general or respected senator. Sometimes there had to

be a civil war between several generals before the new emperor emerged.

Which system do you think would have been the best—election of an emperor from many choices or inheritance from parent to child? What are the advantages of each system?

5. Suppose that you are a general in Gaul in AD 138. You have just learned that the emperor Hadrian has died. You want to be emperor, but you do not want to march your army to Rome because there is a rebellion in Gaul and it would be dangerous to take your army away. Instead, you write a letter to the senate in Rome. You tell them how good you are as a general and what your plans are for the Roman Empire. Read over the career of Hadrian and write down four ways that you think you can improve the government of the empire when you are the emperor.

■ *A Hun invader from Asia. These horsemen from the East swept into Europe and attacked the colonies of Rome.*

outsiders, they now belonged to the official religion of the Roman Empire.

Constantine decided to rule from the eastern part of the empire. He built the new city of Constantinople on the site of the old city of Byzantium. To build the city he taxed the empire very heavily. We know that he personally directed the building of a circus for games, 2 theaters, 6 public baths, 4 government grain storehouses, 6 aqueducts, 12 churches, and 10 palaces. Before Constantine died, Constantinople rivaled Rome in size and importance.

From this new eastern capital Constantine was able to handle the problems of the invasion of the barbarians coming down from southern Russia. Later, in 476, Rome was completely overrun by these invaders from the north. The eastern capital of Constantinople was able to continue for nearly another thousand years. It was not until 1453 that the Turks captured this capital city of Constantine.

Write and Discuss

1. The triarius is in one way better protected than the principes. However, the principes are protected better in another way. Can you see the differences in their protective armor?

2. In what way are the principes better protected than the veles?

3. Why do you think the veles wears a wolf's coat?

4. How many small spears does the veles have ready to throw?

5. What will the veles use to defend himself if the enemy gets close to him?

The Roman Army

The Roman army had the reputation of being the most effective force in the known world. It was the Roman army that gained the empire for Rome. The wealth of slaves, gold, wheat, and taxes that flowed to Rome was forced from the colonies by the Roman army. The Roman army was behind every Roman emperor as the power behind the throne. This army could be used to raise up a Roman emperor or remove an emperor. The Roman army was the best-organized army in the world. Its discipline and organization were so superior that it could win battles even with a bad general. Some modern armies have been patterned on the ancient Roman army.

The Early Roman Army

In the early days of the Roman Republic (500–200 BC), every Roman male adult was a part-time soldier. Every summer, the citizens were assembled at the Capitol Hill for selection. About one in four had to serve for one year. Each citizen-soldier had to supply his own equipment and weapons.

There were four types of foot soldiers in the early republican army. There were the **velites** (the frontrunners), the **hastati** (the first line), the **principes** (the second line) and the **triarii** (the third line). Look at the illustrations of each of these soldiers.

■ *A veles of the velites resting before he is sent into battle.*

■ *A principes soldier of the second line. The hastatus of the first line looked similar except the hastatus carried two throwing spears.*

■ *The triarius veteran soldier waits with his heavy spear. He will only be used if the front lines fail in their attack.*

Write and Discuss

1. What was the advantage of fighting without armor like the velites?

2. The hastati (spear soldiers) carried two throwing spears. If they were advancing and were in the act of throwing their first spear, what do you think they would do with their second spear?

3. The principes (second line soldiers) also carried a light spear or javelin. At what stage in the battle would they be likely to throw these javelins? Would they throw them past or over the hastati in front?

4. The triarii (third line) carried a four-meter heavy spear that they did not throw. How would this heavy, long spear be useful if the first two lines were losing and falling back?

5. If you were conscripted into the Roman army for a year's fighting, what line of the army would you prefer? Give reasons for your choice.

The battle formation of this army was as follows:

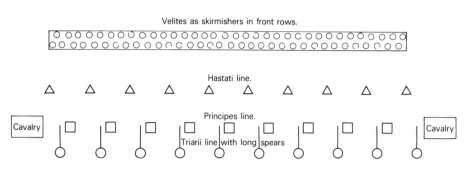

Velites as skirmishers in front rows.

Hastati line.

Principes line.

Cavalry

Triarii line with long spears

Cavalry

Battle Tactics

The battle usually followed the same pattern. The Roman soldiers did not need orders. They were trained in the steps of battle so that they acted automatically. The battle formation of this army was as follows:

- *Step One.* As the Roman army advanced, the velites would move out way in front of the main army. The velites would shout and throw spears and rocks at the enemy. If the enemy showed signs of fear, the young, lightly armed velites would draw their swords and attack the front line of the enemy.

  Usually the enemy would advance through the velites. The velites would melt back through their comrades' lines or retreat out to the sides where they would have the protection of the Roman cavalry, which usually waited on the wings of the foot soldiers' lines.

- *Step Two.* When the Roman hastati were about 20 meters or 60 feet from the enemy's front lines, they would throw their light spears and then, as they got closer, throw their heavy spears. The spears were made so that the iron part would bend on impact. This made it impossible for the enemy to pick up used spears and use them against the Romans.

  The hastati would run forward, get in close, and hack with their short swords. The principes would move up and fill the gaps when a hastatus was killed.

- *Step Three.* The Roman swordsmen got in close and smashed their way through the center of the enemy lines. Using their shields and their swords together, they cut their way through. There was a strict rule of no left-handers allowed in the front line as left-handers would unbalance the cutting machine.

- *Step Four (a).* Once the hastati and principes had broken the center of the enemy line, the enemy would be cut into two sections and surrounded. If the enemy began to run away, the Roman cavalry and the lightly armed velites would chase them.

■ *Step Four (b).* If the hastati found the fighting hard or began to lose ground, the principes would move up through the spaces and use their swords. As a last resort, the triarii were ordered up. These were men over 30 years old, veterans of warfare. They were steady and experienced enough not to run away. The triarii were the back line who steadied the front lines and prevented panic or retreat. Usually the triarii would win a hard battle or could be trusted to fight to the last man.

Defeating the Roman Army

The strength of the Roman army was in its lines that could not be broken. There was always a defense to cover any gaps that were made. However, a brilliant general from Carthage in North Africa thought of a way to beat this Roman army. At the battle of Lake Trasimene in 217 BC, Hannibal used elephants to break up the Roman line formation. In this battle, Hannibal completely defeated the Romans.

A year later at Cannae, Hannibal used another tactic to defeat the Romans. He knew that the Romans would attempt to break through his center line, so he told his center to retreat, still keeping the line together. The Roman principes and surviving hastati followed the bending enemy line. Soon the Romans found themselves inside a trap with the enemy around them. Hannibal then ordered his cavalry to swing around and block off the Roman retreat. The Roman army was completely destroyed. The diagram shows Hannibal's tactics.

■ *The hastati meet the enemy. The two leading hastati come to grips with the enemy front line. One has his sword in action while the other hastatus is throwing his second spear.*

Activity

You are an enemy commander in chief about to meet the Roman army. You know their tactics. You know the Roman strength of discipline and organization. You also know the Roman weakness of never changing their tactics. Without copying Hannibal's ideas, work out a way to defeat the Roman army.

Possible Tactics

1. A line of shields to take the spears of the hastati

2. Long, heavy spears similar to those of triarii

3. Bow and arrow

4. A trench or obstacle fence to stop the Roman advance

5. Charging cavalry

6. Longer swords

Write down your secret instructions to be sent to your army commanders. These instructions could include a plan or diagram.

Write and Discuss

1. Why would a permanent army be needed, rather than a temporary one each year?

2. What are the modern names for some of the Roman colonies of the empire?

3. Compare this map with the previous map of the empire. What new colonies were added after 40 BC?

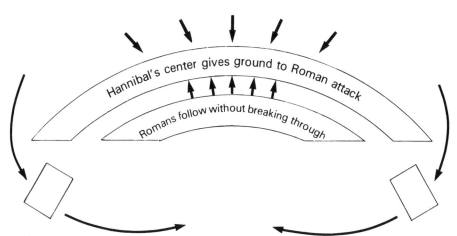

Hannibal's center gives ground to Roman attack

Romans follow without breaking through

Hannibal's cavalry swings around to encircle the Roman army from the rear.

The New Army

By 100 BC, the old army of the republic was no longer enough to guard the Roman Empire. The old-style citizen force was enough for fighting near Rome for a few summer months; however, the empire was now spread out so far that a permanent army was needed. The map shows the Roman Empire just after the Roman army was made a permanent, fully paid army.

■ *Roman Empire 40 BC.*

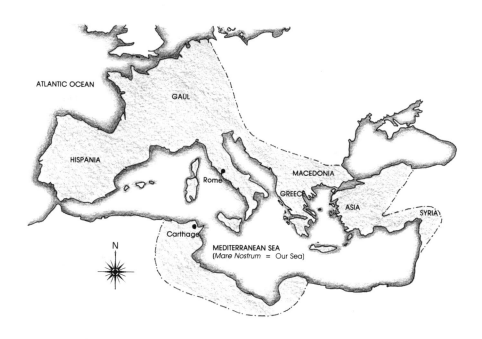

ATLANTIC OCEAN

GAUL

HISPANIA

Rome

MACEDONIA

GREECE

ASIA

SYRIA

Carthage

N

MEDITERRANEAN SEA
(*Mare Nostrum* = Our Sea)

Write and Discuss

1. Why was the Roman army finding it harder to get richer people to join the army? Why would poor people want to join the Roman army?

2. In what different ways did the new Roman legionary get paid?

3. When a legionary retired, the Roman government paid him off with a grant of land in the outer colonies of the empire. How did this method help the Roman government in times of future wars?

4. The officers of a Roman legion were made up of politicians who were gaining knowledge of the Roman army, as well as full-time professional officers. Which officers were full-time officers of the army? Why would the men look to them rather than the political officers in time of battle?

5. Which army would you rather join—the old Roman army of one-year men or the new professional army of full-time soldiers?

In about 107 BC, Gaius Marius, a Roman consul, reformed the army so that it suited the new times.

1. Soldiers now joined the permanent army for 25 years as full-time professional soldiers.

2. Not only property owners but any Roman citizen could join the new Roman army, no matter how poor that citizen might be.

3. The old divisions of different types of soldiers were done away with. All soldiers were **legionaries** with full armor and mass-produced helmets and swords.

4. Soldiers were paid as full-time soldiers. They were given bonuses and a share of any captured booty. At the end of 25 years, the legionary was paid off with land in the colony where he was serving.

5. The legionaries' equipment was no longer carried by slow wagons. Each legionary carried his complete kit on his back when he marched.

6. The army was expanded as a permanent army to about 10 legions with each legion (5,500 men) divided into 10 *cohorts* (500 men).

■ *The New Army.*

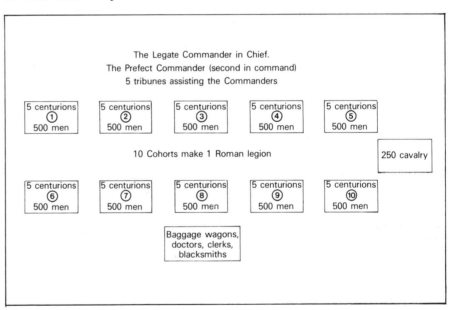

Ranks of Soldiers

Legion commander—A Legate (*Legatus*). A senator appointed by the senate. He would have military background but was a politician as well as a soldier.

Prefect (*Praefectus*).   Second in command to the legate. The prefect was a full-time soldier with up to 30 years' experience.

Tribunes (*Tribuni*).   There were usually five tribunes to a legion. They were young politicians appointed by the Roman senate to gain experience in the army. They were not regarded highly by the legionaries.

Centurions (*Centuriones*).   There were five centurions to every cohort, each centurion in charge of 100 men. The centurion usually came up from the ranks and was the backbone of the Roman officers. The men feared and respected the centurions.

Legionary.   The common legionary signed up for 25 years. He was not supposed to marry so that the army was his life. All legionaries were trained and equipped the same. They were close to the perfect fighting machine. When they retired, these veteran legionaries settled down in the colonies with their families. If war broke out in a far-off colony, the veterans could be called up for duty in an emergency.

■ *A centurion of the Roman army. Note that the plume on a centurion's helmet went across his head rather than front to back as for other soldiers.*

Write and Discuss

1.   Why was this officer called a centurion?

2.   How is the centurion's protective armor superior to the legionary's?

3.   How would you recognize your centurion officer in the middle of a battle by looking at his helmet?

The Professional Legionary

The new Roman legionary was a well-trained professional. He could march 30 kilometers or 19 miles a day, and up to 50 kilometers or 30 miles a day if a forced march was called for. This was done with over 35 kilograms (over 75 pounds) of kit on his back. In addition to a day's marching, a legionary had to make a camp with tents and camp fence every night and cook two meals a day. The illustration shows a Roman soldier on the march.

■ *A Roman soldier on the march.*

The legionary carried all his weapons plus a pick for digging trenches. He also carried cooking equipment, three days' rations, and a leather ground sheet, plus two sticks that were to be used in building a picket fence around the camp each night. For rations he carried wheat, bacon, cheese, and wine. Eight legionaries slept in one tent. Each group of eight had a mule to carry their tent and any extra equipment or rations.

These soldiers did not depend on transport, kitchens, or other support forces. They were almost self-sufficient, or independent. If they were cut off from the main force or caught out in bad weather, a Roman soldier could manage on his own.

As well as being a sword soldier, a Roman legionary could build bridges or build his own camp walls and ditches. When attacking cities, the Roman soldiers were experts in using siege machinery to capture the city.

Many of the Roman roads throughout Europe were built by Roman soldiers so their legions could march quickly to emergency situations.

Activity

The Roman army is an immense topic with whole books written about it. Choose one of the following topics and explore it further:

- Julius Caesar, a great general

- Roads and bridges built for the Roman army

- Hadrian's Wall

- The gladiators of Roman sport

- Hannibal of Carthage, Rome's deadly enemy

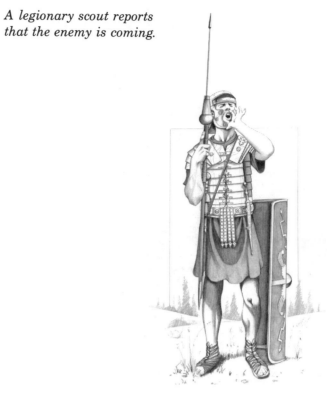

■ *A legionary scout reports that the enemy is coming.*

The End of the Roman Army

The Roman army won much territory for the Roman Empire. At first, only Roman citizens fought as legionaries in the Roman army. These men were loyal to Rome and to the generals who led the armies to victory and wealth. The velites or auxiliaries were the lightly armed soldiers from the outer empire. They might be Syrians, Egyptians, Britons, or Germans. After 25 years of service, these "helper" soldiers were given a diploma of bronze that gave them Roman citizenship. Their sons could become Roman legionaries. The photograph shows an actual diploma. Here is an English translation of another diploma.

The emperor Caesar Vespasian Augustus, pontifex maximus, of tribunician power for the fifth time, saluted as victorious commander 13 times, father of his country, consul five times and designated for the sixth and censor;

to the cavalrymen and infantrymen who are fighting in six squadrons (I Flavia Gemina, I Cannenefatium, II Flavia Gemina, Picentiana, Scubulorum, and Claudia nova) and 12 cohorts (I Thracum, I Asturum, I Aquitanorum veterana, I Aquitanorum Biturigum, II Augusta Cyrenaica, III Gallorum, III and IV Aquitanorum, IV Vindelicorum, V Hispanorum, V Dalmatarum, and VII Raetorum), and are in Germany under the command of Gnaeus Pinarius Cornelius Clemens, who have served for 25 or more years, and whose names have been written below;

has granted to them, to their children and their descen-

Write and Discuss

What rights did the soldier gain from a diploma?

A bronze diploma of Roman citizenship. Courtesy of The British Museum.

dants, citizenship and legal marriage with the wives they had when citizenship was granted to them or, if they were single, with the ones they might marry later, limited to one wife each. 21 May, in the consulship of Quintus Petillius Cerialis Caesius Rufus and Titus Clodius Eprius Marcellus, both consuls for the second time;

to the ordinary soldier Veturius, son of Teutomus, a Pannonian of the Scubuli squadron, whose officer is Tiberius Claudius Atticus, son of Spurius.

Source: *The Use of Documentary Evidence in the Study of Roman Imperial History*, B. W. Jones and R. D. Milns, Sydney University Press, 1984.

The soldiers from Rome were not keen to spend long years away from home fighting on the borders of the empire. This led to a shortage of soldiers. In the second century the laws were changed to allow non-Romans to fight in the Roman army. The number of auxiliary troops from Roman colonies was increased to make up a full army.

When the Roman army was under great pressure, the officers could not always depend on their men to fight to the end. Many of the soldiers were foreigners fighting only for money, not for loyalty to Rome. Once this stage was reached, the Roman army had lost its fighting ability. By AD 300, the age of the Roman army was over.

Roman Houses

Most ordinary Romans lived in *insulae*, which means "islands"—a block of flats. The buildings were four or five stories high, built of clay bricks with clay tile roofs.

They were noisy places, as the bottom story was reserved for shops and workshops. The emperor Augustus restricted them to six stories as many people were being killed in building collapses. The poet Martial lived in one of these city flats; this is what he wrote:

How can I sleep with doors
slamming all night
And then before light, the clanging
of the blacksmith below and
the tap tap tap of the silver smith
The flare of lights, the voices and
laughter, I am going mad in this
place—truly a mad house.

■ *An* insula *in Rome. Most ordinary Roman citizens lived in such blocks.*

Write and Discuss

1. How many people could live in such a building?

2. What would be the problem of living in the middle of an *insula*?

3. How did the Romans protect their *insulae* from the hot summer sun?

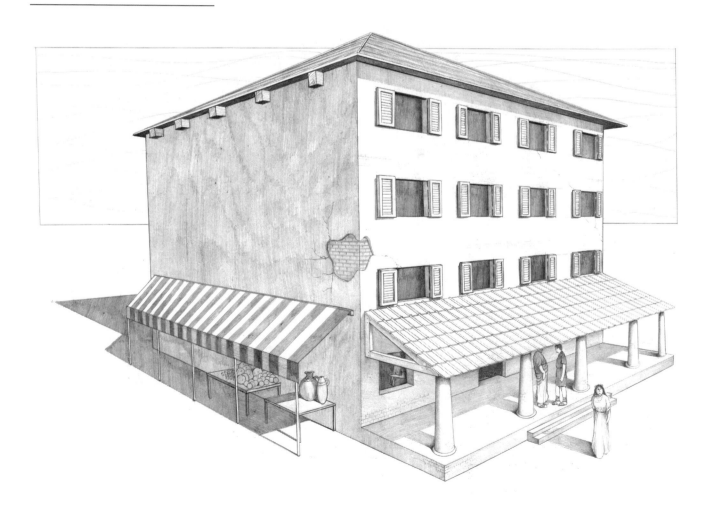

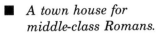

■ *A town house for*
middle-class Romans.

In wealthier parts of Rome, middle-class Romans lived in town houses. These were usually no more than three stories. There were shops below but not workshops or noise pollution.

In the suburbs, Romans built a *domus* or home for themselves. These single-story houses usually had similar floor plans. There was always an atrium or patio in the middle of the house. This center courtyard made a private garden for the family.

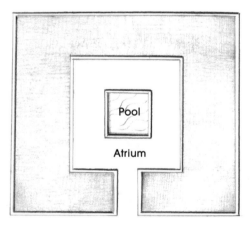

■ *Basic floor plan for a*
domus.

■ Cave Canem—*beware of the dog! Even nonreaders could understand this warning.*

CAVE CANEM

Activity

Rich Romans employed architects and designers to plan their villas and gardens. Draw your own plan of a Roman garden. Romans favored straight lines, stone pathways, trellises with vines, and rows of trees. Romans liked shaded walkways and a mixture of fruit trees and other trees and shrubs.

There was a security gate at the entry to the domus. Near Pompeii, a mosaic tile was found on the front gate of one domus. For those who couldn't read *Cave Canem* (beware of dog), there was the picture of the fierce dog to convey the message.

In the country, a wealthy Roman might build a villa or country home with a garden. Such a villa might need 10 slaves to maintain the house and garden. Usually the Roman owner spent the hot summer weeks or times of plague or disease in this villa. It was a place of escape from the city of Rome.

In the Roman provinces there were many farm villas. These were not holiday homes but real country homes and farms. Such farm villas might employ 20 to 30 slaves.

■ *A Roman country villa
with a garden.*

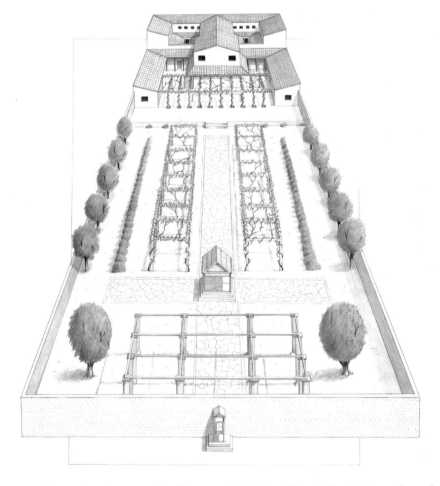

Write and Discuss

1. What sort of vine do you think is growing in the garden?

2. Why do you think there is such a high wall around the property?

Write and Discuss

1. Why might the British villa need so many separate buildings?

2. What are the differences and similarities between a Roman villa near Rome and a Roman villa in Britain? Why do you think the differences occurred?

Look at the picture of a Roman-British villa. It had stone foundations with a stone wall all around. The walls were built of timber and plaster with slate tile roofs. This method of plaster and timber was kept up for many years. The Tudor-style houses built 1,500 years later looked similar to this.

■ *A Roman-British villa
used as a farm.*

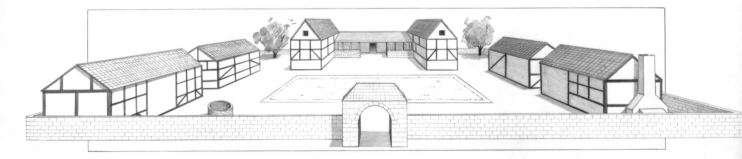

Activity
Write out the following summary of Roman houses in your notebook.

Roman Houses

Ordinary people in Rome lived in blocks of flats called _____.
Life was not very peaceful in these city flats because the whole of the bottom floor was used for _____.

Middle-class Romans liked to live in a *domus* or home. These homes always had a central courtyard. This open space was useful because _____.

Wealthier city Romans liked to own a country villa. A villa always had a ____ attached to it for outdoor living. The farm villa was built for use, not for looks. It had a security wall around it, possibly to keep out ____. Some of the outer farm buildings were used for _____ or _____.

Around Rome most buildings used _____ or _____ for the walls and _____ tiles for the roof. In Roman-British villas they used _____ and _____ for the walls and _____ tiles for the roof. This was because close by they could obtain materials from forests, lime pits, and slate quarries.

Roman Entertainment

Many ruins around Europe show that the Romans were involved in fun and games. Every Roman town had public baths where people went every day to wash and meet friends. There were many amphitheaters for open-air plays and concerts. There was the Circus Maximus where 230,000 people often watched chariot races. There were stadiums for the staging of games and fights between gladiators.

Public entertainment was necessary if emperors or consuls wanted to keep the people on their side. Several Roman writers wrote that the Roman people were no longer interested in the good government of the country. All they wanted was free food, and plenty of circuses—and that is what they got. In the first century AD, the people of Rome got 150 holidays a year. On most of these days there was free public entertainment. This entertainment was on a large scale. The following forms of entertainment would be included.

Gladiators

Gladiators were often slaves and criminals who were trained to fight in special schools around Rome. A good gladiator could expect to live about two years. Most of them were killed in their first few appearances in the arena. Most gladiators wore a masked helmet and some form of armor. They used a short sword called a *gladius*, after which they were named. Some gladiators used a net and a forked spear; they tried to throw the net over their opponent and then skewer him with the trident. Sometimes there were single combats between gladiators. Sometimes there were "wars" between gladiators with packs of up to 200 in one event.

If a gladiator was wounded it was up to the crowd or emperor to decide his fate. If the gladiator had put up a good show, it would be thumbs up—let him live. Thumbs down meant kill him.

This cruel sport made the Roman crowds less than human. Seneca, the famous writer, wrote

> I always come away from the games less of a man
> than I went in.
> The horrible screaming crowd
> shouting out for death
> is unworthy of human beings.

■ *The end of a gladiator—one of the cruel sports that Romans enjoyed.*

Activity

A famous gladiator named Spartacus led a revolt against the Roman government. He organized an army of gladiators and defeated a Roman army. Look in an encyclopedia or history book and see what details you can discover about his slave revolt.

Write and Discuss

The Romans were civilized people yet they cheered when people killed each other and roared with joy when a lion jumped on a running criminal.

1. Why do you think the Romans were so cruel?

2. When people look back on Americans in the twentieth century, will we be known as kind people or will we also be seen as cruel?

Animal Hunts

Another cruel "sport" for the crowds were animal hunts. Animals of all types were trapped in North Africa and shipped to Rome. These included tigers, elephants, leopards, panthers, and crocodiles. Sometimes gladiators hunted these animals in the Colosseum. Sometimes the animals fought one another. At other times criminals or Christians were hunted by the animals and killed. In AD 107, the Emperor Trajan had a whole year of celebrations to praise his victories in war. In six months more than 6,000 wild animals were killed in hunts in Rome alone. By AD 300, most wild animals were extinct in northern Africa and the Middle Eastern countries. They were to be found only in central Africa and India.

1. Which type of Roman entertainment would you like to have gone to? Give reasons for your choice.

2. Why did the Roman emperors give so many free shows to the Roman public? Why was "bread and circuses" good business?

3. What is the link between *gladius*, meaning "sword," a gladiator, and gladiolus (flowers)?

4. How did the Romans keep clean if they did not have soap?

5. Romans went to the baths not just to bathe but also for other reasons. What other things could they do at the baths?

Public Baths

Every town in the Roman Empire had public baths. The Romans did not have soap or running water in every house. Therefore every day they went to the public baths to wash. In Europe the cold weather made it impossible to bathe in cold water so the baths were heated by a furnace system under the baths.

The bather paid a small fee to enter the baths. Male and female bathers did not use the same baths. If there was only one public bath, they went at different hours.

The bathers first took off their clothes in the changing rooms and rented a towel. They then went to the *tepidarium* and bathed in the warm water. Then they went to the *caldarium* or hot, steamy room. Here they took a quick dip in the hot bath. They then had olive oil rubbed on their skin and the skin was scraped with a scraper. This scraped off any dirt from the surface of the skin. The bather then had a quick dip in the cold bath, called the *frigidarium*.

The bathers sat around and talked to neighbors or perhaps had a ball game in the courtyard. There were always slaves to massage them or get their clothes. If the bathers had plenty of time, they went through the routine a few times during one visit. The baths were places to wash, meet friends, gamble, and have some exercise. Most people went there in the same way that people today go to spas or restaurants.

■ *Roman baths.*

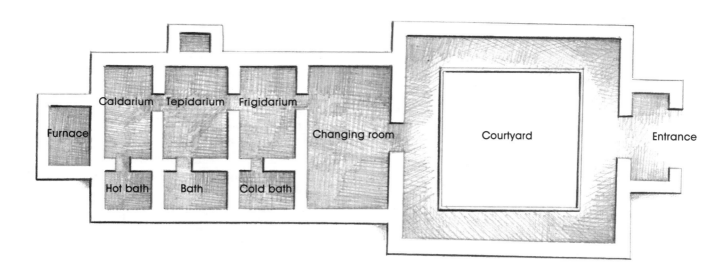

Activities

1. You have been to Gaius Marius Terentia's feast. He doesn't know half the modern foods we have now. Plan out a menu for a surprise party for him. After this party, Roman menus will definitely look old-fashioned.

2. Design a poster for a gladiator fight at the Colosseum. These are the details that you will need to know to design the poster. These posters will be put up around town.

Names of two gladiators in main event: Publius and Cato

Their weapons:
gladius = sword
rete = net
tridens = fork
When? Ninth of September = *novem Septembris*
Where? Colosseum
"Everybody come!" in Latin = *Venite Omnes!*

Design a weapon or helmet on the poster.

Roman Feasts

The richer Romans often had dinner parties for their friends. For some of them it was important to show off how rich they were. They had dancers, and some even had gladiators fighting during their dinner.

The diners did not sit at tables or on chairs. Instead, a series of couches were lined up around three sides of a table. The guests lay on the couches and reached out to the table for their food. Many feasts turned into displays of gluttony. At such feasts greedy guests went outside where a slave helped them vomit. After recovering, the eater returned to the table to start eating again. Seneca, the Roman writer, must have seen this, as he wrote, "Even the pigs know to stop eating when they have had enough."

A typical menu of a Roman feast might look like this:

Gaius Marius Terentia invitat
Gaius Marius Terence invites
Te ad Sumptuum Repastum
you to a lavish feast
Decem Novembris
on tenth of November

MENU

Wine and olives served before sitting for dinner

Course I
eggs and salad *or* shellfish and oysters

Course II
Bream or haddock fish served with
fish sauce & vinegar

Course III
Seasoned grilled sausages *or*
Stuffed roasted mice (yes, mice!)
Bordeaux wine from Gaul

Course IV
Boiled lamb with leeks and onions

Course V
Roasted sucking pig *or*
Roasted veal with pepper and oil
Moselle wine from Gaul

Course VI
Roasted goose with bread

Course VII
Stuffed fried dates *or*
aniseed pastry with honey

Course VIII
Fresh fruit—African figs, pomegrante,
Syrian plums, Egyptian dates.
Red Campania wine from Italy

Guests are requested not to spoil the feast by storing food in clothes
to take home as a hamper. On request, the slaves will collect a
hamper of food from the serving plates *after* the feast. These
hampers will be discreetly given to guests' slaves as they leave.

Words of Wisdom

The Romans were people of action and achievement. However, there were some who looked at other Romans and themselves and spoke out when they thought something was wrong. Others wrote down their ideas on Roman life and where they were going as a people. These people were called **philosophers**, meaning "lovers of wisdom." There were other writers who were poets or writers of plays. They sometimes criticized and laughed at Roman customs and ideas.

Their writing tells us a lot about Romans. Some of their ideas are fresh and alive even after all these years. Below are a few of them. Read them carefully and see if you understand the Romans a little better.

Ausonius was a university teacher who later went on to become a consul. He was born in Bordeaux in Gaul (now France), which was a part of the empire. This is some of the advice he gave to his students:

> All you young girls gather roses while they and you are young, for life will end soon enough.

> Do not look around for company. Mixing with large numbers always brings harm. They will end up converting you to some wickedness. Even when you are not aware of it the tar rubs off on you.

Terence was a Roman slave from Carthage in North Africa. He was brought to Rome and earned his freedom as a writer of plays. This is what he thought of Rome:

> God made the fields and nature. Man made the town and all its dirt and grime.

The next writer, Seneca, made the mistake of becoming the emperor Nero's teacher and adviser. Nero grew tired of him and ordered Seneca to commit suicide.

> Just remember when you are feeling superior that your slave comes from ancestors like you; that slave breathes the same as you, and you die the same as he does.

> Even in peacetime the Roman soldier tires himself out in practicing tactics so that when the time comes he will react automatically. He has to be trained to react in this way. It won't just happen.

Juvenal, like Seneca, lived dangerously. He criticized emperors and made fun of them. Luckily for him he lived to the ripe old age of 70.

Don't start gossiping about a favorite of the Emperor. If you do, you know what your fate will be. You will be up there on the lamp-post blazing away in tar like a human torch. They will drag your blackened corpse off out of the stadium. So shut up— no gossip.

Juvenal did not have much patience with parents of his students:

Parents of students make impossible demands of the teachers of their children. He must be perfect in all subjects and know everything. They will stop you in the street and expect you to have all the answers there and then—impossible people.

Tacitus was a lawyer and a writer. He worked his way up from tribune to consul. He lived through some of the dangerous years of Nero and wrote histories of the emperors and their lives. His father-in-law was governor of Britain, and Tacitus spent some years in Germany. Here are his thoughts on Britons and Germans:

A British captive said of the Romans: the Romans are the greediest, cruelest people on earth. They kill us and rob us and call it government. After they have destroyed a town and leveled it to the ground, they say they have brought peace to the area.

■ *A British captive is led off by a Roman soldier. Such prisoners would be sent back to Rome to be sold off as slaves.*

Write and Discuss

1. What is the advice that Ausonius gives to young girls?

2. Do you think Ausonius gives good advice to his students about mixing with other people?

3. Seneca certainly knew the secret of success for the Roman army. What was the key to their success according to Seneca?

4. Juvenal must have seen some dreadful sights at some of the games in the stadium. What did they do to some poor people?

5. Tacitus sees the victory of the Roman army from the loser's point of view. What is peace and good government to the Roman winner is something quite bad for the defeated Briton. How does the defeated Briton see it?

6. Several of the Roman writers write about death. What is their idea of death? How do they see it? Do they have hope of another life after death? Is death a bad thing for them? What advice do they give about facing death?

7. The Roman Empire lasted for abut 500 years. This is a long time when you consider that the British Empire lasted only 200 years and was the largest in world history. How was the Roman Empire able to last so long?

Compared to Egypt, however, the Roman Empire did not last very long at all. What were the factors behind the downfall of the Roman Empire?

Activity

Listed below are the names of some of the barbarians that attacked the Roman Empire and eventually destroyed it.

- Huns from Asia
- Franks from France
- Saxons from Germany
- Vandals from Germany
- Visigoths from Spain

Two famous barbarian leaders were Alaric and Attila. Look these names up in a reference book. See what each did to weaken the empire.

The Germans shout and scream out when they attack. The result is either to frighten their enemies or they end up terrifying themselves.

Marcus Aurelius was a Roman emperor for many years. For most of his reign he fought the Germans and the barbarians to the north of the empire. Even though he was very busy, he wrote his meditations or ideas. His general idea was that nature is the best guide of how to live.

Nothing can happen to you in this life that your human nature cannot handle.

Do not live as though you had a thousand years ahead of you. Death is close by all the time. Work hard at life while you still have the chance.

Catullus was a young poet who died of the plague in Rome at the age of 29. Like many Roman writers, he was interested in death and what happens after death. Like many Romans, he was pessimistic and believed that when you died there was just blackness—no heaven or afterlife.

When suns go down they rise again. But when our short light has flared and gone, the night for us goes on and on.

Chapter Six

China

Land of History

The Sleeping Giant

Today China is known as one of the greatest nations on earth. With over 1 billion people, China contains about a fifth of the world's present population. More and more people are discovering China as an important trading nation and a powerful nation in the world struggle for power.

China has often been called "the sleeping giant." Napoleon the Great warned the world not to waken the giant. Until this century, European nations thought that China was a backward country, but that was not the case.

China was not a sleeping giant. China has always been awake and active. It is just that Westerners have gotten to know China only during the past 50 years.

The Size and Variety of China

The first thing to understand about China is its huge size. It is a country of mountains and rivers. The mountains have kept the parts of China very different, by separating people from each other. The

Write and Discuss

China has widely differing climates and vegetation. What are these differences?

rivers have always been the home of the Chinese. Along these rivers the Stone Age farmers grew their crops and journeyed up and down in riverboats.

Because of the great differences in climate, people living in different parts of China have always led very different lives. Even today, many people still grow the same kinds of crops that their ancestors grew thousands of years ago. The climate still affects how people live in the different regions.

In the far north of China, north of the Huang He (Yellow River), the Chinese people are nomadic herders. They live on the grasslands and icy hills with their horses and sheep.

In the lowlands of the Yangtze River, Chinese farmers use irrigation to grow rice and vegetables. Despite floods, these people usually are able to live quite well.

In the south of China, the climate is tropical. Here all types of fruit and sugar cane are grown. An important crop is tea.

Farther up the rivers in the dry northwest, Chinese farmers grow wheat and barley.

■ *A Chinese farmer greets a trading boat on one of the great Chinese rivers.*

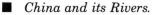 *China and its Rivers.*

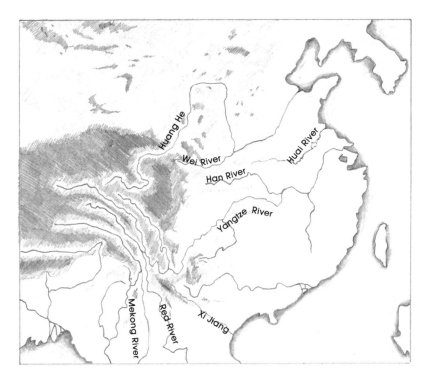

🪨 The Early Dynasties

China has a very long history. We can easily trace the story of the
Chinese people back to 1700 BC. However, when we talk of China at
that time, we are not talking of one united China. There were many
different Chinese kingdoms. China was too large for one king to control.

As in Egypt, the Chinese kings ruled in families or dynasties. In the
earliest times only the most important dynasties were remembered.

Shang Dynasty

During the Shang dynasty (1766–1122 BC) the Chinese became skilled
in the use of bronze. There are still bronze bowls and dishes from this
period.

The Shang kings ruled the land between the Huang He and the
Yangtze River. They were often attacked by the Huns, who were an
Asian people from north of the Huang He.

Zhou Dynasty

The Zhou dynasty (1122–256 BC) began the system of **feudalism**. This
was a system where a warlord ruled over a section but accepted the
king as the supreme ruler of the whole kingdom.

The First Emperor of China

In 221 BC, Shi Huangdi of the Qin state in northern China defeated the last of the feudal warlords. He set himself up as the first emperor of the whole of China. He built a new palace at Hsienyang on the Wei River. Qin became the name of the new dynasty.

Emperor Qin did not want to use feudal lords to govern sections of his territories. He knew that one of them would get too powerful and challenge him as emperor. So he took all the land from the lords. Qin ordered the lords to come to his capital where he gave them work to do. To gain further control, Emperor Qin ordered all brass spears, arrows, and chariots to be surrendered to him. He collected all this brass and melted it down to make statues in his palace.

■ *Shi Huangdi, first emperor of China.*

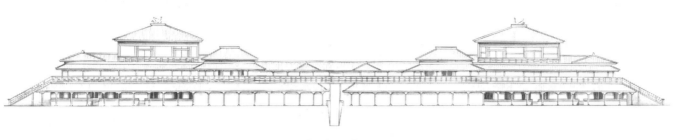

■ *Emperor Qin's palace at
Hsienyang.*

He now had the problem of running this huge empire. Qin developed the "scholar system." A huge number of public servants were trained to be governors and officials for the emperor. They were paid by the emperor and depended on the emperor for their jobs. These scholars took 15 years to train for their first job in the public service. The first thing they had to do was learn the Chinese alphabet, which then had over 3,000 characters or signs.

Running an Empire

There were still many people in the outer section of the empire who wanted to go back to the old system. The farmers did not like paying taxes to an emperor in a far-off capital. They liked to have a local lord. Emperor Qin decided that he must destroy the memory of the past. He must make a fresh start. The emperor called in all the books of learning—everything that recorded the past. He collected all the books and burned them in one big pile.

Some of the scholars tried to smuggle books out of the palace and escape. Nearly 500 scholars were arrested and buried alive for trying to keep books about the old days. After the death of the emperor a few books were found that had survived the fire. Copies were made of these before it was too late. Some scholars cheated by writing fake books of their own and then claiming that they had discovered a famous old book.

Emperor Qin's capital city was on the Wei River. It was often attacked by the Huns from the North. These northeners were nomadic herders who moved from area to area. Qin encouraged his people to become farmers on the river. He moved many Chinese southward as farmers. They were easier to control as farmers rather than herders.

To protect the empire from these continuous raids from the north, Emperor Qin built the Great Wall of China. He appointed General Meng to supervise the task. This huge wall stretched for 2,500 kilometers (over 1,500 miles) across China. Over 3,000,000 peasants worked to build the wall, which had forts all the way along it.

Write and Discuss

1. How did Emperor Qin control the feudal lords once he had defeated them in battle?

2. Why did Emperor Qin try to burn every book in the land?

3. What tricks did Li Ssu use to increase his own power after the emperor died suddenly?

In 210 BC, Emperor Qin died while on tour through the empire. His prime minister, Li Ssu, kept the news of the death a secret. Li Ssu sent commands ahead to the capital in the emperor's name. Li Ssu's rival generals and the heir to the throne were ordered by the "emperor" to commit suicide. When the caravan arrived back at the palace, Li Ssu's enemies were all dead and Li Ssu was able to put another weaker son on the throne.

On the way back to the capital it was becoming obvious that the emperor was dead. The servants kept taking food to the emperor's caravan every day, but after several days they refused because of the smell. Li Ssu ordered a cart full of dead fish to travel in front of the emperor's caravan. After a few more days of travel, the smell of rotten fish blotted out everything else.

■ *The Great Wall of China.*

The Tomb of the Emperor

The emperor died suddenly before his tomb could be completed. We know that thousands of workmen were working on his tomb because an old Chinese book has left us this record.

The King's Tomb

As soon as the First Emperor became king of Ch'in [in 246 BC] work was begun on his mausoleum at Mount Li. After he won the empire [in 221 BC], more than 700,000 conscripts from all parts of China laboured there. They dug through three underground streams; they poured molten copper for the outer coffin; and they filled the burial chamber with models of palaces, towers and official buildings, as well as fine utensils, precious stones and rarities. Artisans were ordered to fix automatic crossbows so that grave robbers would be slain. The waterways of the empire, the Yellow and Yang-tzu rivers, and even the great ocean itself, were represented by mercury and were made to flow mechanically. Above, the heavenly constellations were depicted, while below lay a representation of the earth. Lamps using whale oil were installed to burn for a long time.

The Second Emperor decreed [in 210 BC] that his father's childless concubines should follow him to the grave. After they were duly buried an official suggested that the artisans responsible for the mechanical devices knew too much about the contents of the tomb for safety. Therefore, once the First Emperor was placed in the burial chamber and the treasures were sealed up, the middle and outer gates were shut to imprison all those who had worked on the tomb. No one came out. Trees and grass were then planted over the mausoleum to make it look like a hill.

Source: *The First Emperor of China*, Arthur Cotterell, Macmillan, London, 1981.

Guards of the Tomb

In 1974, some Chinese farmers were digging a well about two kilometers (a little over 1 mile) from Emperor Qin's tomb. They discovered a life-sized statue of a Chinese soldier. Scientists were called in. To

■ *The buried army of the emperor. Each of these clay soldiers had a different face.*

Write and Discuss

1. Why were thousands of clay soldiers buried with the emperors?

2. What other ancient country buried statues of soldiers with their kings?

3. What is the archaeologist in the picture doing?

their surprise they found the buried army of Emperor Qin. When he died, 7,000 clay statues of his army were buried in battle formation next to the tomb.

The soldiers had generals in front of them. There were clay horses and chariots as well. Each one of the 7,000 Chinese soldiers had a different face. When we look at them we are looking at replicas of actual soldiers in Qin's army.

End of the Qin Dynasty

Even though Qin had been a powerful emperor, his dynasty lasted only eight years after his death in 210 BC. He had pushed the people too hard and too fast. He had stopped the old feudal way of life. He had forced people to work on huge public projects, such as the Great Wall. Qin had started taxes to pay for his new public service. A peasant army took over and killed Qin's successor. The army also broke into one of the pits where the statue army of Emperor Qin was buried. They smashed the statues and stole the crossbows and spears to use against the emperor's son.

The new dynasty that took over was known as the Han dynasty. It had more luck than the Qin dynasty. The Han dynasty lasted for 422 years, from 202 BC to AD 220.

Chinese Inventions and Improvements

Many people regard the Western world as the leader in new ideas and inventions. This is not really true. The Chinese nation has led the world in many improvements and inventions.

Silk

Silk is one of the finest natural materials in the world. Today, nylon material can be used for making sheer stockings and light materials in scarves and dresses. Before nylon came into use in the 1950s, silk was the finest material that could be used. It was literally worth its weight in gold.

The Chinese first learned the secret of making silk. An early empress learned to grow mulberry trees for the silkworms. She also invented the process of spinning and weaving the fine silk thread from the silk moth's cocoon.

Fine silk material found its way to Europe across the overland silk routes that spread to India and the Middle East by 100 BC. The Chinese were able to keep the process of producing silk a secret until AD 550. Persian traders then smuggled some silkworm eggs out of China in a hollow bamboo. Soon a rival silkworm industry sprang up in Constantinople.

■ *The silk routes.*

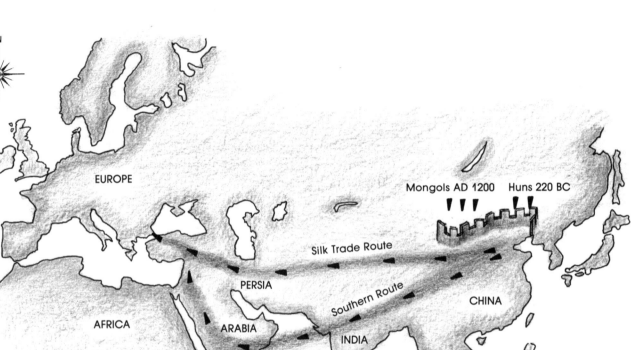

Paper

The Egyptians and early Hebrews used papyrus to write on. In Europe before AD 1200, important books were written on linen cloth pages. Important documents were written on vellum, which was specially prepared calf's skin that would not rot easily.

The Chinese developed the art of making glossy heavy paper in the second century BC. They later developed the art of making very thin rice paper. In AD 751, Arab Muslims captured several Chinese papermakers, who taught the Arabs the art of making paper from old cloth rags and flax plants. Most Arabian books were soon written on paper. The Arabs introduced paper into Spain and Sicily in the twelfth century. By 1450, paper was in popular use throughout Europe—an invention imported from China through the Arabs.

Printing

When paper became plentiful in Europe, a method of printing books on paper quickly followed in the 1400s in Germany. With only 23 letters in the German alphabet, wooden and metal blocks were easy to make so that words could be printed. The task for the Chinese printer was much harder, because the printing press would have to deal with the thousands of letters that made up the Chinese alphabet. For this reason printing in China was never as cheap or widespread as in Europe.

However, in the same way that knowledge of making paper came from China, the art of printing may have come along the trade routes.

The Chinese first used paper to make ink rubbings from Chinese writings carved in stone. The Chinese made wooden stamps by the second century BC. They covered these with ink and stamped the white paper by hand. By AD 500, the Chinese were able to print paper money, playing cards, and posters by pressing paper sheets on inked carved wooden blocks.

In 1043, Bi Sheng cut from clay several thousand alphabet blocks that he was able to arrange by hand in a metal frame. This was the first use of movable type, 400 years before Europe developed the system with an alphabet of only 23 letters.

■ *Bi Sheng the printer, 1043. Chinese printing was invented hundreds of years before printing in Europe. Most Chinese printing was for posters and government notices. Red and black were favorite colors.*

The Chinese did not improve on Bi Sheng's printing press. The job of making thousands of different letters and sorting out the puzzle on a printing frame was too slow. Scholars chose instead to write their letters and books by hand. However, the Chinese must be said to be the pioneers of modern printing on paper.

Pottery and Porcelain

The Chinese were the first to glaze pottery. This means they put a hard, shiny, water-resistant surface on the pots and jars by heating them in high-temperature ovens. This meant that instead of using metal cups and plates they could use their porcelain pottery to eat from. The food did not stain the plate and was easily washed off after meals. By 1700, European traders were importing Chinese pottery as the best in the world. Even today people talk of *china* when they refer to porcelain dinner sets.

As well as using porcelain for practical purposes, the Chinese developed the art of making high-quality decorative vases and porcelain statues long before the German and English potters copied them in the eighteenth century.

■ *A painted porcelain vase of the Ming dynasty, 1510.*

The Power at the Top

There have been many dynasties of emperors in China over the last 4,000 years. There also have been many rebellions that have ended the dynasties. But until 1911, the rebels never started a new form of government. Even when peasant leaders defeated an emperor they always started a new line of emperors. That is how strong the idea of emperors was. When the emperors were in power their power was supreme.

One of the most remarkable emperors of all was Empress Wu.

Empress Wu

The Tang dynasty was very powerful in the seventh and eighth centuries. In 638, Wu was chosen as a wife of Emperor Tang Taizong. She was only 13 years old when she joined the emperor's other 120 wives. In 649 the emperor became sick and was about to die. Wu knew that her life at court was about to end. She and all the other wives of the dead emperor would be sent to a Buddhist convent. There she would spend her years as a nun.

Wu risked death by falling in love with the emperor's son, Tang Gaozong. (It was strictly forbidden for an emperor's wife to have a lover.) When the old emperor died, Gaozong became the new emperor. All of the old emperor's wives, including Wu, were sent to the convent. It looked like Wu was doomed.

But then a miracle happened. The new empress was jealous of one of Gaozong's younger wives, and she did not want the son of the number two wife to become the next emperor. The empress discovered that Wu had been Gaozong's secret love, so she had Wu released from the convent. Soon the emperor had forgotten his number two wife and was deeply in love with Wu.

But the empress's plan did not work as well as she had hoped. Soon Wu made her move to become empress herself. She accused the empress of murdering her (Wu's) newly born baby. For this, the empress was dismissed as the emperor's wife. Wu then became the first wife of Gaozong. But there was a real problem in getting Wu accepted by the royal family. Both Gaozong and Wu could be executed for breaking a basic taboo of Chinese law—Wu had married two emperors.

■ *Empress Wu listens to her court favorite.*

Activity

Many of the emperor's ministers protested to the emperor. They knew the true story of where Wu came from.

Imagine that you are one of the emperor's advisers. You are writing a petition to the emperor telling him why Wu cannot become the new empress. In your petition you must remind the emperor of the truth about how Wu came to the palace.

Your petition will be very different from the emperor's edict. Remember, however, that the emperor has the power of life and death. Your petition must be in the most polite terms. It could start like this: "Your most celestial and Royal Highness. Though deserving a thousand deaths for approaching your throne with this petition, I must for your sake beg you to reconsider your decision. . . ."

The emperor was very powerful, however. He made an announcement about Wu that was untrue:

> The Lady Wu comes from one of the most famous families of China. She was chosen to come to the palace because of her talents and high virtue. Her main job was to look after the emperor's mother. Lady Wu was always by the side of the mother of the emperor. The old emperor noticed how good she was. He constantly praised Wu and gave her presents. Then the old emperor gave Lady Wu to our present emperor, Tang Gaozong.
>
> Because of her devoted service it is right that Lady Wu be raised to the level of empress.

The Chinese court knew that this was a false story, but they dared not say anything publicly. Wu was crowned as empress.

As empress, Wu busily worked at revenge against her enemies. All those who spoke out against her were executed for plots against the emperor. When Gaozong became sick, the Empress Wu took over more and more as the real ruler of China. Under her direction, the country of Korea was conquered and came under Chinese control.

When the emperor died in 683, Wu stopped any of his sons from becoming the new emperor. Empress Wu was able to handle the plots against her life by being one step ahead of them. When she could, she demoted Gaozong's sons to commoners and sent them into exile as minor officials. In many cases when her own life was in danger, she was forced to execute them. Empress Wu was able to rule China with a rod of iron for another 20 years. This was remarkable in a time when women in China normally were not given any power or authority.

In 690, Wu reached the peak of her power: she was crowned as the emperor of China. The Chinese could not accept a female monarch. They could not crown her queen or empress. The idea was too foreign. But Wu was so powerful that she was accepted as emperor.

Finally, in AD 705 at the age of 80, the Empress Wu was deposed from the throne. Unlike many of her victims, she was not executed. She was allowed to die in peace a few months later. Wu is still remembered as the only woman ever to become the emperor of China.

The Great Wall of China

The Great Wall of China is a huge structure that stretches across the north of China. It is 6,400 kilometers (about 4,000 miles) long. The picture shows the eastern part of the wall near Beijing. This section is still preserved in good condition as an example of what the wall was like. In other parts there is only a faint outline left of where the wall used to be. Satellites orbiting over China have photographed the Gobi Desert, and the photographs show the outline of where the wall used to be.

Why Was the Wall Built?

The Great Wall was begun in the time of the Emperor Qin, who was the first emperor of all China. This was in the years 200 to 210 BC. To the north of the Huang He were the grass plains of Manchuria and Russia. The people there were known as *Huns*. They were a nomadic people, moving around with their horses and sheep. The Chinese emperor wanted to protect his people from the Huns, who sometimes swept down from the north and raided the cities. Every summer he sent armies north to patrol the borders. The armies set fire to the grasslands to deny the Huns feed for their horses.

The idea of a wall was the answer to the raids. This first emperor built a wall only hundreds of kilometers long. Over the centuries other emperors added sections to it to keep out the northern invaders.

As well as being a barrier to keep out foreigners, the wall was to keep in the Chinese. The Chinese emperors were trying to control huge numbers of people. The northern grass plains were areas of free-

■ *A gate fortress along the Great Wall of China, near Beijing. This part of the wall in eastern China is still in good condition.*

dom. The emperors did not want their people to have this choice. They wanted the Chinese to be farmers and be settled in one place where they could be controlled. The Great Wall of the north was a sign that the Chinese were locking out the other world while the emperor built up the country of China.

A European traveler who saw the wall early in this century wrote:

> The walls have protected Chinese civilization for all these centuries. The walls have finished their task. They can now crumble away. The Chinese race has its own inner defenses of their strong civilization. No foreign invader can destroy this Chinese way of life for many long years.

Write and Discuss

1. Who was the original builder of the Great Wall? When was the Great Wall enlarged?

2. Why was the Great Wall built?

3. Who were the people who broke through the Great Wall?

The Second Wall of China

In 1215, a new threat came to the Chinese from the north. The feared Mongols were from the same area as the Huns. Their leader was Genghis Khan. He broke through the wall in the western part where it was not as high and strong.

Activity

Walls are of great interest and importance to people. They are built for various reasons. Here are three walls that you could research.

- Hadrian's Wall in northern England
- The Wailing Wall in Jerusalem
- The Berlin Wall in Germany

Find out what they are and why they were built. Are there any other famous walls in the world? A clue—city walls of cities like London or Rome.

Activity

The Huns from the north of China were feared by the early Chinese emperors. List four reasons why the Huns were feared by the Chinese.

Genghis Khan's horse soldiers found it difficult to capture the Chinese cities and towns. Sometimes they camped for three years outside a city before they starved the people into surrender. Genghis Khan is credited with this clever plan, which is recorded in Chinese chronicles:

> The city of Limin held out for six moons. The Mongols promised the town people freedom if they would sign a piece of paper. The Chinese agreed to hand over all their cats, swallows, and pigeons. These were caught and carried out to the Mongols through the city gates.
>
> The Mongol general collected all the animals and placed the burning fire [phosphorus] on their tails. He released the animals, and the creatures, maddened with pain and fear, rushed back inside their hometown. That night the wooden buildings burned down as the burning animals had brought destruction to the town. The Mongols easily captured the burning town that night. No living thing was left alive.

Genghis Khan's grandson was Kublai Khan. He captured Beijing and started a new dynasty of Mongol emperors. This Yuan dynasty was at first popular because it was kind to the peasant farmers. They welcomed the Mongol rulers from the north. But the Yuan dynasty was overthrown in 1368 by a peasant revolt. A peasant leader started a new dynasty known as the Ming dynasty.

- *Hun invaders.*

The Ming dynasty was to last almost 300 years. Its first task was to push back the Mongols. By 1400 this had been achieved. The emperor Zuh Yuanzhang set about isolating China from outsiders. He undertook rebuilding the Great Wall.

Organizing the Labor

Zhu Yuanzhang's general, Xu Da, divided the wall's 6,000 kilometers into nine districts, with an engineer general in charge of each district. The soldiers were employed as workers. At any one time up to 400,000 soldiers would be working on the wall.

The peasants of each district were forced to work for several months each year. They were used to working on big projects building canals and flood control walls along the Huang He. Convicts or prisoners were sent to work on the wall. They were given the hardest sections over the snowy mountains and across the deserts in the west.

Organizing the Materials

The builders usually used local materials rather than carrying the material for long distances. In the western plains the builders used rammed earth walls. These walls had sloping tops with tiles on them

■ *A cross-section view of the Great Wall of China.*

Activity

Draw or trace the cross-section diagram of the Great Wall in your own notebook. Label the details of the wall on your drawing. These are the wall's specifications:

8 meters (24 feet) high
9 meters (27 feet) wide at the base
5 meters (15 feet) wide at the top
Rubble central core
Stone outer foundation blocks
Clay brick upper wall
Clay tile top roadway

so that rainwater would run off. Most of the tiles have washed away over the years.

In the east, near the sea, the builders used wood from the forests to build watchtowers along the wall. The timber formed the top part of the walls as well as housing for the soldiers.

Most of the Great Wall was built of stone, rubble, and bricks. A cross section of the wall is shown in the illustration.

The clay bricks, the mortar, and clay tiles were made close to the wall. Donkey carts and donkeys were used to carry the tiles and bricks. The stone blocks were cut in quarries and in hilly areas and were passed along a human chain. Each stone was passed about 1,000 meters (over 100 yards) through thousands of pairs of hands.

Two clever inventions that were used on the wall were the Chinese wheelbarrow and the "endless chain," or conveyor belt. Unlike the Western wheelbarrow, the Chinese barrow had a wheel in the center. This wheel formed the center of gravity and allowed one person to transport a much heavier load than the modern Western wheelbarrow.

Write and Discuss

What modern machines are based on this Chinese invention?

■ *The "endless chain."*

Defense Measures

All along the Great Wall were towers with beacon fires ready to be lit should there be an attack. Chinese soldiers slept in small towers along the wall. These could be reinforced from regularly spaced garrisons along the wall. Reinforcements marched on the road along the top of the wall.

At regular intervals along the wall were gateways to allow traders, travelers, and armies to go through. Each of these gateways had an extra fort built into it as special protection for a weakness in the wall. These gateways varied in style, depending on the building styles of each district.

Activity

As the Great Wall stretched to the west, the gates in the wall became plainer and simpler. Which of the gates in the illustration would be found in western China?

Suppose you are a Chinese architect in far western China. You have been given the task of designing a gate. The gate must have a simple fort or defense works above it so it can be closed and defended against an attacker.

Draw your gate. It should be simple, cheap, and useful for defense.

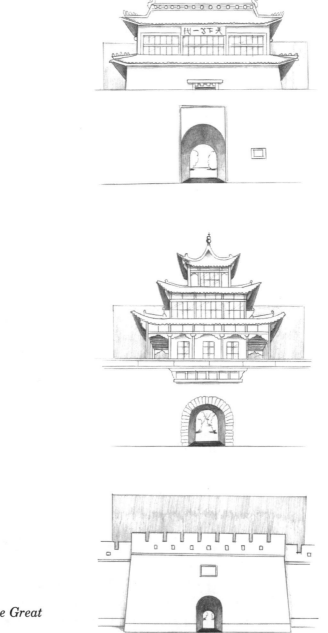

■ *Three gates in the Great Wall of China.*

The End of the Wall

For 250 years the Great Wall stopped the northern invaders. Finally, in 1644, Manchu invaders broke their way through the wall and captured the Chinese capital, Beijing. These northern Manchus set up another dynasty, the Qing dynasty. As they came from the north themselves, the new Manchu emperors did not keep up the defenses on the Great Wall. Instead of being afraid of the northerners, the new Chinese dynasty encouraged trade and contact with the northern tribes. By 1800, the northern invaders had come under Chinese control.

The Great Wall was to be of little use to the Chinese in the future. The new threat to China began to come across the sea in ships from Europe. No walls could keep these new invaders out.

Invaders from Europe

The Chinese had knowledge of other countries through their western overland trade route. By 140 BC this trade route had developed westward to the Mediterranean Sea. From China the Romans learned the secret of making silk. In return, the Chinese imported grapevines, beans, and pomegranate trees from Persia and the Middle East. In the eighth century the Arabs brought back from China the art of glazing porcelain tiles and the art of making paper.

China was far by sea from the rest of the world. Chinese ships traveled along the Asian coast as far as India and Africa. They followed the islands south as far as Indonesia and possibly visited Australia. At all times the Chinese emperors were in control of the trade. When they wished to cut off trade by sea or land to the west, they could do it because the distance was so great.

In 1274 an Italian explorer, Marco Polo, reached China on the overland route. He lived in China for 14 years. He became a friend of the Mongol emperor Kublai Khan and served as a governor of a province for four years.

Marco Polo returned to Italy by sea. On his way back he visited Indonesia and India. When he arrived home nobody believed his stories of the Chinese rockets with gunpowder that flew up in the sky. The people did not believe that there could be an unknown emperor in a place called *China*. Marco Polo found himself in jail, where he wrote a record of his stay in China called *The Book*.

The pope in Rome was interested in China. He sent missionaries to China by the silk route. By 1350 there was an archbishop in China, and for a time Christianity was popular. By 1400 both China and Europe knew about one another. But they were so far apart that they were not greatly interested in keeping close contact.

All that changed in the 1500s and 1600s. The Portuguese and the Dutch broke through to Asia with a new ship that could travel far across the seas. This new ship was the **caravel**, a sailing ship that could sail even with the wind against the ship.

The Chinese emperor was interested in trade. The Europeans began to buy large quantities of Chinese tea and Chinese silk. The Portuguese were allowed to set up a permanent trading port at Macao on the South China coast.

Matteo Ricci—An Italian-Chinese

Another remarkable European arrived in China in 1582. His name was Matteo Ricci. Ricci was a highly educated man with great knowledge of mathematics, physics, and astronomy. He was sent out as a Jesuit missionary to convert the Chinese to Christianity. Ricci thought that the best way to convert the Chinese was to aim for the emperor, so Ricci went to Beijing to try to see the Ming emperor.

The Chinese could not believe that a "barbarian" such as Ricci could know so much about astronomy. Ricci helped the Chinese reorga-

■ *Matteo Ricci.*

nize the Beijing Observatory on a modern European basis. Ricci also became the official cannon maker for the Chinese emperor. At this time the Ming emperor was being attacked from the north and the use of cannons was very important to success. Ricci showed the emperor's craftspeople how to cast bronze cannons that would fire cannonballs without self-destructing.

Matteo Ricci dressed in Chinese fashion and spoke only Chinese. He wrote 20 books in Chinese and made many Christian converts among the nobles of Beijing, although he was never able to convert the emperor. When Ricci died in 1610, he was given a tomb in the imperial grave section.

Matteo Ricci was admired by the Chinese because of his great learning. He did not act superior to the Chinese. Instead, he adopted their ways and their language. In their history books the Chinese gave him the compliment of special mention and had a Chinese name for him—Li Madou.

Write and Discuss

1. Why didn't the people of Europe believe Marco Polo's reports about China?

2. Matteo Ricci, the missionary, was accepted by the Chinese court. There were several reasons for this. Name two of them.

3. Why did the Chinese emperor expel all Europeans from China in the 1600s?

The Europeans Expelled

The missionary work of Matteo Ricci did not live long after him. A new Chinese emperor did not like Christian missionaries working against the Chinese religions of **Confucianism** and **Buddhism**. All missionaries were expelled.

In the south, the Spanish and Portuguese traders were expelled from China. These traders were becoming too pushy, and the Chinese emperor did not like being ordered about by men from across the sea.

Only the Dutch were allowed to stay on one small island near Guangzhou (Canton). They were regarded as honest traders, and they did not make great efforts to convert the Chinese.

The Europeans Return

By 1800 the European countries were going through an age of expansion. They needed raw wool, silk, and cotton to use in their factories. Countries like Britain were looking for new markets for the goods from their factories.

The British king sent his envoy to China to tell the Chinese emperor that he wished to trade with his country. This is the answer that George III of England received from the Chinese emperor:

> You, O King of England, have heard of our greatness and wish to do homage to me. You have sent us presents. I will send even better presents back to you.
>
> Know, O King of England, that we Chinese do not need any of your goods. We have all the things to make us great. There-

fore I cannot allow you to open up trade. I cannot allow your
envoy to live in our city of Beijing.

Listen to my orders, O King of England, and obey. We are
pleased with your tribute to us, the center of the world, but
that is as far as it goes.

This time the Europeans could not be expelled. They were too
powerful. Soon the whole of eastern China was opened up to trade.
The ships and powerful guns of the Europeans were too much for the
Chinese. By 1900 China had lost its independence and had become the
victim of outside armies and navies that opened up the whole country
to trade. This trade was good for the European invaders, but it was of
little benefit to the Chinese because of the low prices they got for their
goods.

The Peasant Farmers of China

China is a country of large rivers. The people of China have always
used the river valleys to grow their food. As in Egypt, the backbone
of the country was the peasant farmer. Through the ages there have
been many changes in the way these farmers organize themselves, but
some things have remained the same.

Owning the Land

Peasant farmers sometimes owned 2 to 5 acres of land. Land was
passed down from father to son. Women had little power, although
they shared the hard work on the farms.

If there was a crop failure, farmers fell into debt buying food. In
these cases they lost control of their land to rich landlords. The landlords took maybe 30 percent of the rice at harvest time as their share.
The farmers might have to pay another 20 percent of their rice harvest
as taxes to the emperor. Many peasant farmers lost their land altogether to the landlords because of debt. Then they worked for low
wages or for a small share of the rice crop.

As land was a matter of life or death to the mass of people, there
were sometimes peasant revolts against the emperor. On three occasions a peasant leader of a rebellion became the new emperor after
defeating the old emperor's army.

Watering the Land

The Chinese peasants valued water as the source of life. The Chinese emperors had huge canals built across plains from the major rivers. These canals were used as a source of water to irrigate the rice fields. Water poured into the flat fields to cover the rice plants. As the rice grew, the water gradually soaked into the ground. Because of the irrigation, no rain was needed to grow two rice crops in one year.

In the drier regions Chinese peasant farmers carried water with yokes. The yoke went over the farmer's shoulders and was balanced by two wooden buckets of water. Each plant was watered carefully so that none of the nearby weeds got any of the water and was able to compete with the rice plants.

■ *A Chinese peasant farmer carries water with a yoke.*

Write and Discuss

1. What do modern farmers use for irrigation?

2. What advantage does watering each plant individually by bucket have over other methods?

3. How was the Chan-kuo method of planting superior to planting the whole flat field with rice or wheat?

Growing Crops

Before 100 BC, Chinese farmers practiced **crop rotation**. That meant that they only used one-third of their land at any one time.

	Field A	Field B	Field C
Year 1	crop	grass	grass
Year 2	grass	crop	grass
Year 3	grass	grass	crop
Year 4	crop	grass	grass

About 100 BC, during the Chan-kuo period, a clever farmer worked out a new system. He said that spreading wheat or barley seeds across the fields was a waste. Weeds grew in among the crops, and it was hard to water the food plants unless there was enough water to flood the entire field.

The farmer said the new way to plant was to use all the fields each year but to divide the fields into narrow strips and plow the soil into mounds. This sounds simple, but it was a wonderful new idea for the dry-land farmers of western China.

Plants were grown in the lower drains, where they would collect more water than on flat fields. The farmers walked along the mounds and pulled the weeds without walking on the crops. As the plants grew, soil would wash down around the roots and strengthen them. The next year the farmers would dig new growing drains along the mounds that had just had a rest.

Like the Ancient Egyptians, the Chinese peasant farmers used oxen and a single plow to plow their fields. Poorer peasants used wooden spades or digging sticks. Later they used iron spades.

■ *The new Chan-kuo planting system.*

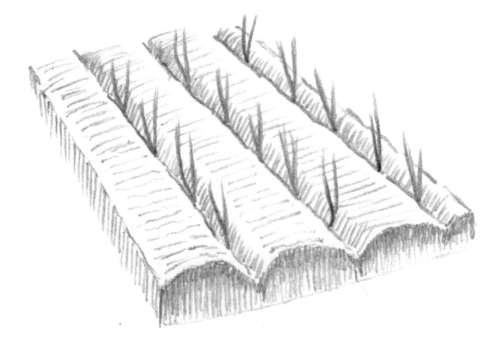

The Chinese Language

Chinese is one of the oldest languages on earth. It is spoken by more people than any other language, even more than English. Two types of spoken Chinese developed. The language of most of China is Mandarin, which is spoken mainly in the northern parts of China. This form of Chinese became the official language of the emperors and their officers. It was the language of government. It was this language that helped to unite the whole of China in the Qin Dynasty of the second century BC.

The other form of spoken Chinese is Cantonese. This form of Chinese is spoken by the people of the southeastern section of the country, around the port of Guangzhou (Canton). Many of the early Chinese immigrants to the United States and Australia were from these southern parts. Many Chinese-Americans and Chinese-Australians speak Cantonese Chinese.

The Development of Writing

Written Chinese was first recorded about 1700 BC. Ancient Chinese writing has been found scratched on bones and carved into stone. After 200 BC, the central government of China was strong enough to make all Chinese use a common form of writing. The standard form of writing has been used since then, although it has been simplified in this century.

Until this century, only about 5 percent of Chinese people could read or write Chinese. Government officials were scholars who had to go through a long period of training. Many years of this training were spent learning the words needed for officials to read and write documents for government purposes.

English is a **phonetic** language. It is based on phonemes, or sounds. The sounds are represented by the 26 letters of the alphabet, *A* to *Z*. New words in English can be formed by combining the sounds that the alphabet letters represent. When people first start to read English, they start with simple words like *cat*. It is only a short step to build on the *-at* sound and learn to read and say *bat, fat, hat, mat, pat, rat, sat,* and *vat*. The spoken and written forms of English are very closely related.

Chinese is a **tone** language. The meaning of a word depends on the pitch used in saying the word. There are four pitches or tones in standard (Mandarin) Chinese. Instead of using alphabet letters, the Chinese developed a different system for writing their language. Written Chinese uses **characters** or signs. There is a different character for every word.

Many Chinese characters are **pictographs**. They look like the objects they represent. Other characters are **ideographs**. They represent ideas. Ideographs sometimes combine several simple characters to create one more complicated idea.

By 200 BC there were 3,000 separate Chinese characters. By AD 100, when written Chinese was used throughout the emperor's government, the number of Chinese characters had increased to 9,000. Most of the early characters were names of objects.

As Chinese civilization became more advanced, the number of objects that needed names increased. Chinese writers wanted to express ideas as well as name objects. In 1716, the Kangshi dictionary listed over 40,000 different characters for 40,000 different objects and ideas. This meant that a Chinese government clerk in 1716 would have to be able to recognize 40,000 different Chinese signs in order to read and write well.

■ *Chinese pictographs—characters that represent things.*

Write and Discuss

In what ways do the pictograph characters look like the objects they are describing?

forest 林   木 tree   grove 森

馬 horse   日 sun

wheat 來   three 三

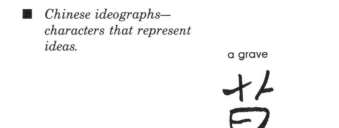

Chinese ideographs—
characters that represent
ideas.

a grave

late

to order

Remember that the clerk did not have a phonetic alphabet like English to sound out a new word and discover its meaning. Like English, many Chinese words looked very similar to other words but had different meanings.

At first the Chinese wrote on bone, wood, and stone. Official documents were written on silk. After the Chinese developed paper they began to write by using black and red inks with brushes. The use of paper and brushes meant a much faster and cheaper form of writing. For instance, people could send business letters or social letters to their friends. They would not write these letters themselves but instead pay a scribe to write the letter. The receiver would then pay a scribe to read the letter. Being a scribe was an important, high-status job in ancient China.

Modern Chinese Language

As long as the emperors used the scholar system to train government servants, the Chinese language remained very complicated. At the beginning of the twentieth century, the Chinese government wanted to make the language simpler so that more people could read and write. This would make it easier to educate the people and modernize China. The number of Chinese characters was reduced to 10,000. The characters were simplified to four strokes of the pen for every word.

Later the communist government under Mao Zedong made the language even simpler. Written Chinese is still very difficult, but over 70 percent of Chinese people can now read and write Chinese.

China Today

China went through many upheavals in the nineteenth and early twentieth centuries. In 1949, after a civil war, Mao Zedong formed the **communist** People's Republic of China. He became the new powerful leader of China. China expanded its industry and worked hard to modernize.

But there were many difficulties. By the 1960s the ruling Communist Party had split over the direction the new China should take. Disagreements led to what was called the "Cultural Revolution," in which thousands of political leaders were removed from office and universities were closed down.

By the early 1970s, the situation in China had settled down somewhat. After many years of isolation, China again opened its borders to foreign trade and diplomatic relations. In 1971, China was admitted to the United Nations.

But in 1976 both Mao Zedong, the leader of the Communist Party, and Zhou Enlai, the Premier of China, died. This led to a power struggle that continues to today. The changes in government have been accompanied by changes in the daily lives of the Chinese people. Many students and young people have demanded that China become a democratic country, with the rights of free speech and a free press. The Chinese government does not want to allow that much freedom. In June 1989, the Chinese People's Army crushed a student rebellion and executed or imprisoned many Chinese who did not agree with the government.

Many western countries like the United States welcomed the way the Chinese government had opened the country to new ideas over the past 15 years. The way the government crushed the student demonstrations in Beijing's Tiananmen Square in 1989 damaged the growing friendship that China was developing with other countries.

1766–1122 BC	The Shang dynasty.
1122–256 BC	_____.
221–202 BC	Shi Huangdi of the Qin dynasty becomes the first emperor of all China.
_____	Han dynasty rules China.
100 BC	Overland silk trade routes to India and Persia established. Chan-kuo farmer _____.
AD 500	Chinese developed printed money, posters, and pictures.
AD 550	Persian traders smuggle silkworms out of China and set up silk trade in Constantinople.
AD 690–705	_____ becomes the only woman to be crowned as emperor of China.
AD 751–1043	Captured Chinese papermakers teach art to Europeans. Bi Sheng the printer _____.
AD 1215	New invasion from the north of China by the _____.
AD 1236–1627	Ming dynasty; emperor Zhu Yuanzhang and general _____ begin to rebuild the Great Wall.
AD 1274	Marco _____.
AD 1582–1610	Matteo _____.
AD 1644	Manchu invaders from the north establish the _____ dynasty.
AD 1716	40,000 characters now in Chinese language.
AD 1800	Europeans come by sea and force Chinese to trade with them.
AD 1900	Chinese government loses all control of its overseas trade to European countries.
AD 1949	Communist revolution under leader _____.
AD 1989	_____.

Activity

Here is a time line of the history of China. All the dates and events are mentioned in the chapter. Copy the time line into your notebook and complete it.

Chapter Seven

The Middle Ages

Into Darkness

The Melting Pot

The United States has often been called a "melting pot." A melting pot is used to heat and melt down metal objects to form a new object. **Immigrants** from all over the world have come together to form a new nation.

There were already about 1 million people living in what is now the United States and Canada when the first European immigrants arrived in the 1600s. Some of the Native American tribes helped the early immigrants grow food and survive in the New Land. But as more and more immigrants arrived and pushed westward, the Indians' way of life was threatened.

The United States saw many waves of immigrants. The first colonies were established in the 1600s by immigrants from England, the Netherlands, and France. Black Africans were brought to America to work as slaves in the colonies. In the 1700s, many German and Scotch-Irish settlers arrived.

After the Revolutionary War, immigration to the United States increased rapidly. Millions of people arrived in the 1800s. In the early 1800s, most of the immigrants were Irish or German. Many Chinese were brought over to work on the railroads. In the late 1800s, poverty and religious and political persecution in Europe brought many more immigrants. Over 13 million people arrived between the 1870s and

Activity

By asking parents and relatives, discover why millions of people have left their homes to migrate to America. Possible answers to your questions will be:

(a) to escape the destruction of war and fighting

(b) to escape corrupt or harsh governments

(c) to get a higher standard of living

(d) to escape overcrowding

Why did your family first come to the United States?

1920s. The immigrants came from the Scandinavian countries, Eastern Europe, and Italy. In the 1900s, many immigrants have come from Mexico, Cuba, the West Indies, and Southeast Asia.

All of these different people have come together in America's melting pot to form the country that is known as the United States. The old ways of the early English and Dutch immigrants have melted down with the ways of the new immigrants from Asia and South America. Over the years the new immigrants will absorb old American ways. But the newer Americans will also keep some of their old ways and add new customs and ideas to the old American mixture. For example, Americans now have many new foods added to their old diets.

Canada, Australia, New Zealand, and many Latin American countries have also become melting pots. Like the immigrants to the United States, the new settlers have introduced new ways into the national life. As the newer immigrants pass through several generations, they add new customs and ideas to their new home and absorb new customs themselves from their new land.

In Chapter 5 we saw how the Roman Empire brought law and order to Europe and the Middle East. This all ended with the destruction of the Roman Empire. We saw that there were several reasons for the downfall of the Roman Empire, and one of these was the invasion and migration of "barbarians" into the empire.

Between the years AD 500 and 800, at the beginning of what is called the **Middle Ages,** Europe became a vast melting pot. For various reasons people poured into Western Europe. They helped to break down the old ways and introduce new ways. From this melting pot came a new Europe with only a few things left from the old Roman days. This is what this chapter is about.

The "Invasions" of the Barbarians

The map shows the movements of new people into Western Europe. The word *invasions* is in quotation marks because the people were migrating rather than attacking. Men, women, and children, with livestock and possessions, poured across the Roman borders around AD 400. As you can see from the map, the natural borders of the Roman Empire were the major rivers.

Along the Danube, the Rhine, and the Elbe rivers, the Romans had built a network of defenses. Wooden fences, towers, forts, and guarded bridges kept the barbarians out. The Romans called these eastern people *barbarians,* but this can be translated simply as "non–Roman." The Romans regarded anything foreign as barbarian and uncivilized, but many of these easterns were not savage people. They had a system of kings and lived settled lives of farming.

The Romans were usually able to keep the eastern raiders in check. The Goths regarded the Romans as superhuman. They could never defeat the Romans in battle. A Gothic king named Athanaric visited Constantinople in AD 381. When he saw the magnificent city with all its wealth and power, he shook his head in wonder.

> I am looking at what I have heard of but I never believed it. Surely the Roman emperor is a god on earth. Whoever lifts his hand against Rome is committing suicide.

The Goths and the Germanic tribes of the north had a healthy respect for Roman power.

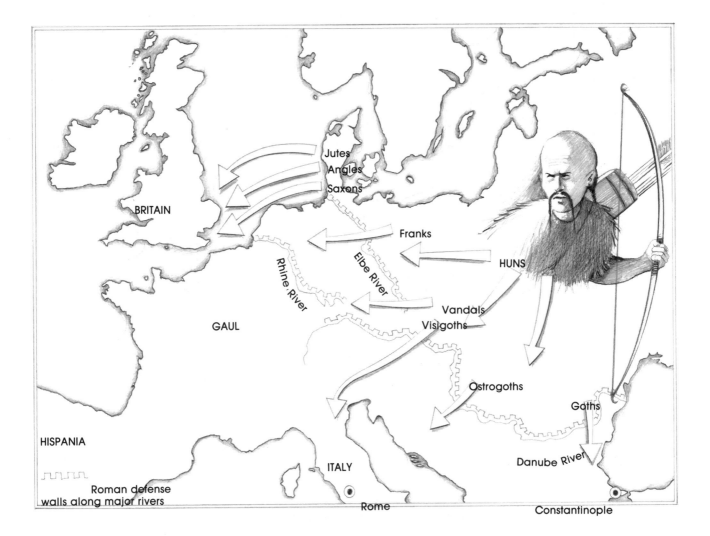

■ *The barbarian "invasion" of Western Europe.*

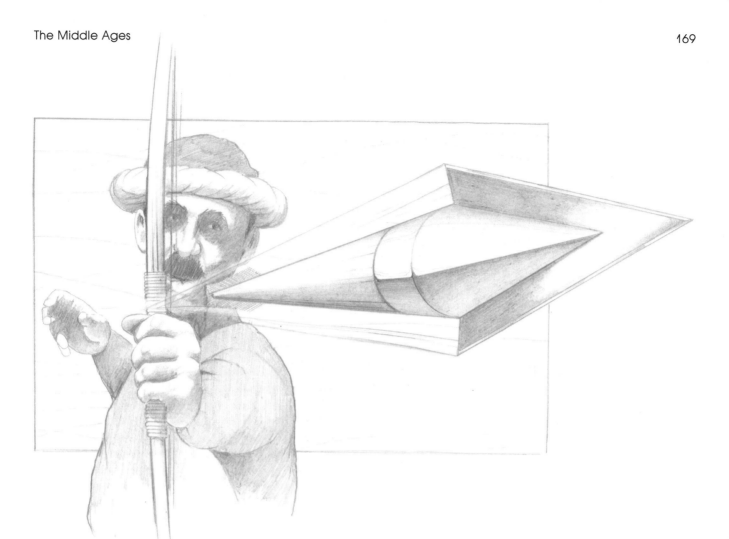

■ *A Hun bowman fires a deadly arrow. The Huns were from north of China. They eventually settled down in Russia and central Europe. Some Europeans known as* slavs *still have the high cheekbones that they inherited from the Huns of 1,600 years ago.*

The First Wave

All this changed in about AD 400. Up to 200,000 Visigoths poured across the Danube River into the Eastern Empire. They told a story of a new people coming from the east. These were the Huns. They were the same Huns that were spreading into China.

The Huns were nomadic herders who followed the grasslands. They lived on horseback and moved swiftly from country to country. The Huns were feared because of their speed and savage attacks.

The Chinese had built their Great Wall and had pushed back the Hun invasion. Now the Huns were forced to spread westward into Russia, Hungary, and Germany. This created a domino effect on the people of central Europe.

To escape the Huns, 200,000 Visigoths migrated across the Danube, defeated a Roman army, and spread into Italy. In AD 410, under their leader Alaric, the Visigoths captured Rome.

The Visigoths were not mad burners and killers. They saw that the Romans lived better than they lived. The Visigoths adopted Roman customs and ways. Some settled down as landowners. Others joined the Roman armies as auxiliary troops to fight the Huns on the river borders. The main body of Visigoths drifted across to Spain where they set up a Visigoth kingdom.

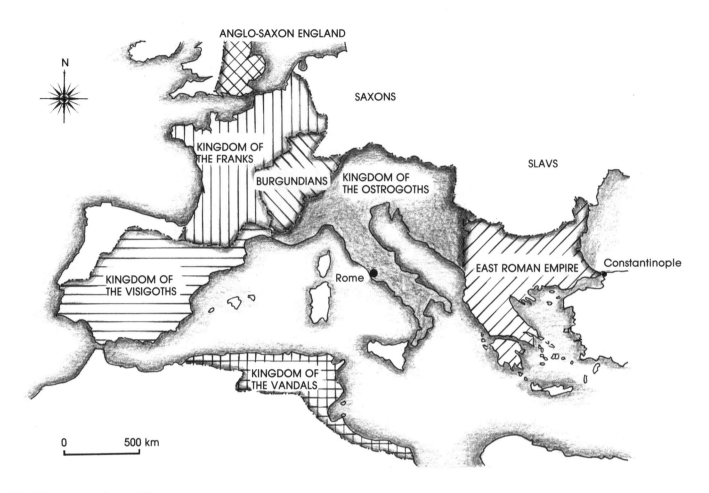

ANGLO-SAXON ENGLAND

SAXONS

SLAVS

KINGDOM OF THE FRANKS

BURGUNDIANS

KINGDOM OF THE OSTROGOTHS

EAST ROMAN EMPIRE

Constantinople

Rome

KINGDOM OF THE VISIGOTHS

KINGDOM OF THE VANDALS

N

0   500 km

■ *The new rulers of Europe.*

The Second Wave

Another wave of barbarians came across the Rhine River in AD 406. These were the Vandals, the Alanis, and the Sueves. The Huns had pushed them out of central Europe. These groups pushed south into Spain.

The Sueves set up a kingdom in northwest Spain. The Vandals and the Alanis moved across to North Africa where they established a Vandal kingdom. The Vandals later sailed back across the Mediterranean in 455 and sacked the city of Rome once more.

Attila, the leader of the Huns, now ruled all land east of the Rhine. In 451 he led an invasion into Gaul (France) and was defeated by Theodoric, the king of the Visigoths. The next year Attila attacked Italy. Pope Leo of Rome went north to meet Attila. He talked to Attila and persuaded him to go back across the Rhine. Probably part of the persuasion involved gold. Attila's favorite method was to threaten attack and allow himself to be bribed off. The emperor of Constantinople, Theodosius II, sent annual caravans of gold across the Danube to buy off Attila.

Write and Discuss

1. Refer to Chapter 5 on Rome. What were some of the things that caused the Roman Empire to decay and fall apart?

2. What were the river boundaries that separated the Roman Empire from the barbarians?

3. What was the basic force that was pushing the barbarian tribes westward early in the fifth century?

4. Describe the three waves of barbarians that swept into southern Europe during the fifth century.

5. What features of the Roman system did the Ostrogoths keep after their king, Theodoric, captured Italy?

6. What countries did the northern Franks and Saxons invade?

7. By the middle of the sixth century, the number of cities and towns had increased in some areas and decreased in others. What two areas of southern Europe now had many cities?

The Third Wave

In 453 Attila died unexpectedly. At his wedding feast (one of many), his nose began to bleed. It could not be stopped, and he bled to death. After Attila's death the Eastern Hun Empire became confused and torn with civil war. This allowed a wave of Ostrogoths to sweep across the Danube. After fighting the Eastern Roman Empire, these Ostrogoths under King Theodoric invaded Italy. Theodoric defeated the barbarian king of Italy and set up his own kingdom.

Theodoric ruled until his death in 526. Instead of destroying all things Roman, Theodoric used the Roman system of government. He kept the Italian public service and even minted coins with his likeness on them, just like the old Roman emperors had done.

In the north of Europe the same process occurred. A Germanic tribe named the Franks moved westward into Gaul. Farther north the Angles and Saxons moved westward by boat and settled in Britain. By AD 540 the face of western Europe had changed completely. Instead of one Roman empire, a series of Germanic kingdoms ruled Europe.

The maps give some idea of the decay of Rome as the center of the world. One map shows the new rulers of Europe. On the other map, each dot represents a city or town of importance in the year 480. Obviously the center of civilization had moved eastward. The Eastern Roman Empire had hundreds of cities and towns with Constantinople as the capital.

In the west only Rome and a few cities remained important. A number of important cities were located in North Africa at that time. North Africa was a thriving and important area.

■ *Important cities and towns, AD 480 (there are no records for Italy and Spain at this time).*

■ *Saxons rowing their ship
to Britain.*

Write and Discuss

1. What is the man at the back of the boat doing?

2. Would such ships follow the coastline or would they row out to sea? Give reasons for your answer.

Saxons, Angles, and Jutes

The northern wave of barbarians was made up of Germanic tribes known as Saxons, Angles, and Jutes. These three tribes traveled westward by ship to Britain. They rowed the ships rather than using sails.

It is not known for certain why these tribes moved westward. We know that they reached the shores of Britain in about AD 400, so they were probably victims of the great Hun migration from the east. Some historians believe that pressure of population forced young warriors to look for new lands to settle. Much of the land of northern Germany and Denmark was made up of sandhills and turf bogs. This poor land could support only a limited population, so migration was the probable answer for these people.

Although most traces of these northern tribes are now gone, some incredible discoveries have been made in this century. Hundreds of preserved bodies have been found in the bogs. The bogs were once lakes. They dried out but were rich in old leaves and vegetable matter. Modern people cut the turf out of these bogs and dry out the blocks. In winter these dry blocks are used to burn in kitchen fires.

In 1950 a turfcutter in Denmark unearthed a complete body of a man. He thought the man must have been murdered, so the police were called in. The scientists from the police department announced that this man from Tollund had been dead at least 1,600 years. He was a perfect relic of the Jutes, from the time when they invaded Britain.

Doctors conducted a post mortem on the body. They said that the body was preserved by the acid in the bog. He was a man of about 30 years of age who had been killed by choking with a rope that was still tied around his neck. The Tollund Man had red hair and wore a leather cap on his head. There were many types of seeds and grasses still in his stomach; two of them were barley and linseed. It is believed that his last meal was a soup made from grasses and seeds. Archaeologists have formed several theories about the Tollund Man.

Write and Discuss

Which of the three theories about the Tollund Man seems to be the most likely? Give reasons for your choice.

1. This ancient Jute man was found naked except for a leather cap. Robbers stole his money and clothes, murdered him, and threw his body in the shallow lake. He is an ancient murder victim.

2. The Saxons and Jutes had fertility ceremonies every spring to make sure of good crops in summer. The Tollund Man was a sacrifice to the Spring Goddess. He was given a last meal of the seeds and grasses that they were growing as crops. The Tollund Man was then choked and sunk in the lake with rocks and branches. He did not struggle or fight but accepted his own death as a worthy sacrifice.

3. The Tollund Man has a calm sleeping appearance, not the look of a man who has just been choked to death with a rope. The Tollund Man died a natural, peaceful death. As many bodies are found in these dried lakes, this must have been the normal way to bury dead people. So he would not float to the top, the Jutes tied a rope around his neck and weighed the rope down with a heavy anchor stone or underwater peg.

■ *The Tollund Man.*

■ *A Saxon farmer digging on his new farm in Angleland (England).*

Ancient Britain

The last Roman soldiers left Britain in AD 410. They were needed to defend the Roman Empire against the Huns and Goths in the east. This was the signal for the wild Picts and Scots to pour over Hadrian's Wall and attack the rich Roman towns in the south of Britain. The Britons had been protected by the Romans and now were easy targets for the invaders. The king of Kent, Vortigern, invited the Jute raiders to help him fight the Pict invaders from the north. The Jutes helped Vortigern but then turned on the British king. The Jutes stayed on in Kent and formed their own kingdom.

The word soon spread to the Saxons and the Angles that Britain was easy to attack. The Roman towns were easy to attack and steal from. The Saxon and Angle raiders found that the climate of southern England was milder than northern Germany. The soil of this new land was also richer than the windblown sandhills of Germany.

The Britons were easy to push back. By 550, much of Britain was captured by these German invaders. The map shows how the country was divided up. There were many Anglo-Saxon kingdoms.

The Anglo-Saxon kingdoms were unified somewhat by religion. In 597 the pope sent a monk called Augustine to Kent in England to convert the king to Christianity. Augustine converted the king and most of his people. Augustine started a monastery at Canterbury. Augustine became the archbishop of Canterbury. Today, the archbishop of Canterbury is the chief bishop of the Church of England.

Activities

1. See what you can find out about the legend of King Arthur. Who were some of the Knights of the Round Table? Where did Arthur and his court live? Who was his queen? How did his kingdom end?

2. Reread the section on Ancient Britain to fill in the blanks in this summary. Write the answers in your notebook.

The Saxons who invaded Britain early in the _____ century were really three separate tribes from northern Germany. The three tribes were the _____, _____, and _____. The last Roman soldiers had left Britain in AD ____ to defend Rome. This left Britain undefended. The British king of Kent invited the _____ to help him defeat the _____, who now poured southward over Hadrian's Wall. The Jutes and later the Saxons and Angles decided to stay as settlers in England. They pushed back the Britons, who escaped to live in _____. The Saxons set up small kingdoms. The three main kingdoms of the Saxons were _____, _____, and ____. In AD 878, ____, king of Wessex, became the main king of England.

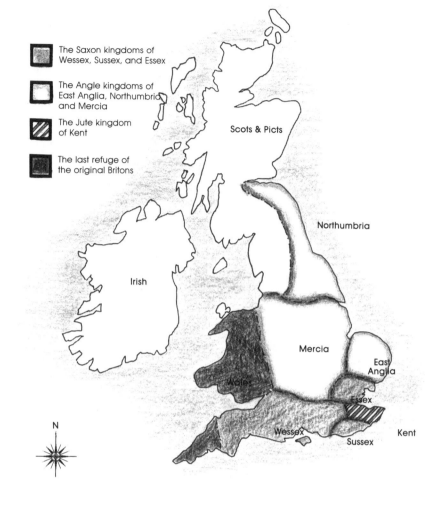

The map legend:
- The Saxon kingdoms of Wessex, Sussex, and Essex
- The Angle kingdoms of East Anglia, Northumbria and Mercia
- The Jute kingdom of Kent
- The last refuge of the original Britons

Scots & Picts

Northumbria

Irish

Mercia

East Anglia

Wales

Essex

Wessex

Sussex

Kent

N

■ *Britain in 550.*

Despite their religion, the Anglo-Saxon kingdoms remained enemies for hundreds of years. Finally, in 878, Alfred, king of Wessex, became the king of all southern England. The southern Saxons became the dominant people in England. Their new land was not called Saxony but Angleland, or England. The new people of England became known as Saxons even though they were Angles and Jutes as well.

What happened to the original Britons? Many of them were educated people from Roman times. Some were employed as advisers to the Saxons in their new lands. Many Britons escaped the Saxon invaders and went to live in the wild hilly country of Wales as free people.

A legend has survived to this day of King Arthur and the Knights of the Round Table. King Arthur was a Celtic king who ruled a small kingdom in southwest England. We do not have any real evidence that Arthur existed, but stories have come down telling how he fought the Saxon occupation of his land. He was eventually defeated and all traces of his kingdom and his brave Britons had disappeared. Only his legend remains.

Activities

1. Some of the words in your dictionary have *OE* after them. This stands for *Old English,* which means that the word was originally a Saxon word. Make a list of 20 words that were originally Saxon.

2. Here are some modern German words. See if you can guess what each word means in English. You will find from this exercise how closely the English language is linked with the German language.

Garten	neu
gut	und
Kinder	unter
Knie	Volk
Kuh	Wetter
Montag	

■ *Invaders and English.*

People	Language	Words
1. Ancient Britons	Celtic	crib, bin, curse, story
2. Roman army (Occupation–AD 410)	Latin	legion, camp, mile, villa
3. Saxon invasion (410–500)	German	woman, and, child, god, brother, the, him, her, his
4. Viking invasions	Danish	law, oak, knife, bread, die, egg, down, kill, take, want
5. Norman French (Occupation— 1066–1450)	French	venison, colonel, assault, siege, justice, honor

The New English Language

The English that we speak and write today is very hard to learn (especially to spell!). This is because English has borrowed many words from other languages. Over the centuries, different peoples have invaded Britain and contributed another layer of words to the English language. The chart lists some of those invasions and the new words that came to our language.

The Saxons brought the basic English language to Britain. The old Celtic language was submerged by the Germanic language of the new Saxon rulers. In Europe, the Saxon language developed into modern German and Dutch. In England, the Saxon language developed into English. Later, Viking words and French words were added to the language, but the original Germanic language remains as the foundation of English.

English Words from the Saxon Language

- ■ *Place names:* Essex, Sussex, Suffolk, Middlesborough, Bolton
- ■ *People's names:* (first names) Edith, Ethel, Alfred, Edmund, Herbert; (second names) Coleman, Godman, Harding, Norman, Sperling, Watman
- ■ *Common names:* sheep, child, children, woman, women, father, mother, folk, hill.

■ *A Saxon farmhouse.*

Write and Discuss

1. Why did such houses have no windows?

2. There were no chimneys in such houses. How did they manage the smoke of fires inside the farmhouse?

A New Way of Living

When the Saxons came to England in the fifth century, they destroyed the old Roman ways. The Romans had a road system, a trade system, and a system of government. We have seen that the Franks destroyed the Roman system in Gaul (France), the Goths destroyed the system in Hispania (Spain), and the Vandals destroyed the Roman system in North Africa.

The Saxon invaders attacked and destroyed the Roman towns in Britain. The Saxons were land-hungry farmers, not educated townspeople. The Saxon kings set up a system of farm living rather than city living.

The kings lived in a fort or castle. The Saxon kings at first controlled a small area. Their chiefs of the tribe became leaders of a village. These villages were new settlements. Saxons did not use the old stone houses of the defeated Britons but built their new houses of wooden poles and grass roofs.

There are no Saxon houses remaining intact today, but archaeologists have built reconstructions of them. The drawing shows what Saxon houses probably looked like. The walls were sometimes made of wooden poles. The Saxons used branches (called *wattle*) and daubed them with mud. This is called a *wattle and daub* house.

A new system of government came to be at about this time. The new system was called *feudalism*. The leader of each Saxon village was called a **thane**. The thane was the largest landowner in the area. The thane was the judge and military leader in case of attack from other thanes. In times of war, the thane would collect his men and march off to help his Saxon king for several weeks.

Write and Discuss

1. Why didn't the Saxons live in the Roman-Briton towns?

2. What were the names of the different classes of people in a Saxon village?

3. What did the Saxons use for building materials?

4. Over a full year, what types of foods did the Saxons eat?

5. The Saxons did not have wire for fences. How do you think they would keep the animals out of their crops?

6. Why did the thane's household have a high wooden fence all around it?

7. Why would the thane need a large barn?

8. Do you think the wives and children of serfs would remain serfs too, or would they be free to leave the thane's village?

In the Saxon village there were freemen known as **churls**. Most churls owned enough land to support their own family. A large village may have had a blacksmith or a woodcutter who was a freeman. Some men in the village were slaves or **serfs**. The serfs belonged to the thane. They owned no land but worked the thane's land.

The Saxons were skilled farmers. They knew how to rest the land so that it did not wear out. They had a three-field system of **crop rotation**. Once every three years, a field was given a rest. This would be the rotation of crops for three years:

Year	Field One	Field Two	Field Three
Year 1	wheat	barley	fallow
Year 2	fallow	wheat	barley
Year 3	barley	fallow	wheat

Each field had long, narrow strips. Every freeman had several of these strips to grow his crop for the year. All the freemen and serfs plowed a field, grew seed, and harvested at the same time. Each strip of land was divided by a mound of earth. This strip farming meant that each man could own his own land but the year's crops were grown on the one field by the whole village unit. With crops like wheat and barley, large numbers of people were needed for harvesting by hand so it was better that they all helped one another and worked as one unit.

As well as the three-field system, the Saxon villagers had other food sources. They kept cattle, pigs, sheep, and fowl. The animals were kept in the rough, hilly meadows. They were also taken into the fallow field where they ate the grass and manured the field for next year's crop. In good years the villagers cut hay in the meadows and stored it to feed the animals in the winter. In bad years they killed most of the animals and salted or smoked the meat to provide food during the hard winter.

The villagers used the forest for building material. During summer they picked the wild berries and during the autumn they collected acrons, chestnuts, and other nuts. Saxon hunters might catch deer, wild pigs, and hares. Hunters used spears, hunting dogs, and nets.

Each village had an area called *common land*. This belonged to everyone. Animals could graze here and firewood could be collected, but no one including the thane could fence the land or build a house on the common. Some English villages still have commons to this day. The commons are now used for sport, camping, or for grazing pet horses or goats.

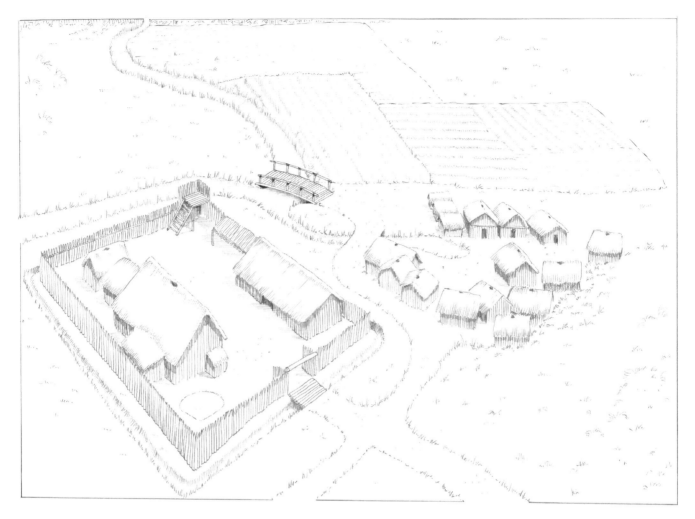

A typical Saxon village of
the seventh century.

Write and Discuss

1. Where do you think
the thane lived?

2. Which area do you
think would be used as
common land?

3. Modern archaeologists have been able to
reconstruct Saxon villages
by mapping out the holes
left in the ground. What
about Saxon buildings
would make this possible?

Europe Settles Down

The barbarians from the east had destroyed the Roman cities and
roads. But even these barbarians had settled down by AD 700. They
lived as farmers in France, Spain, Italy, Germany, and England. These
countries were not large, united countries. They were broken up into
small kingdoms like the Saxon kingdoms of England. The only thing
these small kingdoms had in common was their Christian faith.

Life in **medieval** Europe was very basic. It meant, for most people,
being born in a village, working as a farmer, and living a short, hard
life. Few people went to school or had the chance to improve themselves. Their lives were dominated by two forces. Their thane or lord
was the master. They fought for him in wars and gave up to one-third
of their farm produce to him. The church ruled their spiritual life.
Most of the people looked to their village priest to lead them. This
village priest would take his instructions from his bishop and the pope
in Rome. To this extent the lives of the common people had some sort
of order and direction.

The Monasteries of the Middle Ages

By 700 a new agency was spreading through Italy, France, and England. This was a church called a **monastery**. A Roman holy man called Benedict of Nursia developed the plan that was followed by most of the Roman Catholic church. Men who wanted to serve God joined the monastery and became monks.

Benedict founded his first monastery in Monte Cassino in Italy in 529. Most big towns and cities soon had at least one monastery. Some monasteries had 50 or even 100 monks. The monks wore plain clothes. They lived together in the monastery and spent most of the day either praying or working. After a two-year apprenticeship, monks took a vow to remain for life in the monastery. Benedict set out a rule of life and even a daily timetable for the monks to follow. This is a daily timetable:

2 a.m.	early morning prayer in chapel
3–5 a.m.	sleep again
5–6:30 a.m.	more prayer in chapel
6:30–8 a.m.	porridge breakfast and housekeeping, such as sweeping and washing
8–11 a.m.	morning work
11 a.m.–noon	reading of Bible or holy books
noon–1 p.m.	lunch of bread and wine or beer
1–5 p.m.	afternoon work
5–6 p.m.	prayer in chapel
6–7 p.m.	evening meal of vegetables and bread (meat once a week)
7–8 p.m.	evening prayer in chapel
8 p.m.–2 a.m.	monks retire to their cells

Monks worked and prayed together as a group. The Grand Silence was from 5 p.m. to 7 a.m. Monks did not talk to each other during this time.

It certainly sounds like a tough life. Yet hundreds of monasteries sprang up all over Western Europe.

Benedict made it a rule that each monastery had to support itself and not be a burden on the people. All monks had to work at least seven hours a day. Most of this work was growing their own food and working on the monastery farm. Benedictine monks became expert farmers and passed on knowledge to the peasant farmers. They were especially clever at growing fruit trees and grapevines and at bee-keeping.

Write and Discuss

1. What type of work is this monk doing?

2. The strange haircut of the monk is known as a *tonsure*. Why do you think the monks had a special haircut?

■ *A Benedictine monk at work.*

■ *A letter from an illuminated manuscript.*

The monks helped the ordinary people in several ways. Each monastery had an infirmary for sick people. The monks were experts in herbal remedies but could do little for such diseases as the plague. Each monastery had a gatekeeper. It was his job to welcome travelers and give them shelter at night in a little house at the front gate.

The skilled monks worked in the dayroom. This was a room with large windows to let in plenty of light. Monks worked here on copying books. Printing had not yet been invented, so books were very rare and valuable. The monks spent years of work copying out just one book. They did not use paper but instead used vellum or animal hide for important documents. They took special care with Bibles and holy books. They developed a special method of decorating and illustrating books. Such books are called *illuminated manuscripts*.

When the books were copied they were not put on the shelf and forgotten. They went into the monastery library where they were chained to desks so they wouldn't be stolen. Because of the care taken of them, we still have some of these books 1,400 years later.

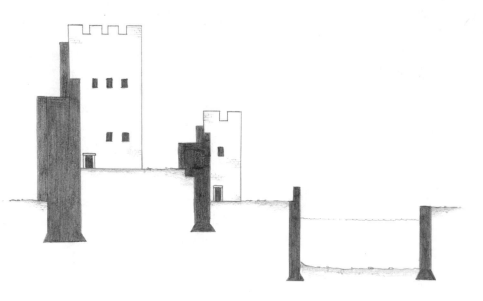

■ *The three walls of
Constantinople. The
shaded parts represent
original walls. The towers
were added by the Norman
crusaders in the twelfth
century.*

Write and Discuss

1. What two forces ruled
the peasant in the village
life of AD 700?

2. Why do you think that
hundreds of young men
joined the new monaster-
ies that spread throughout
Europe?

3. What work did the
skilled monks do in the
dayroom? Why was their
work so important?

4. The Eastern Roman
Empire had some out-
standing people who
helped rebuild the em-
pire. They were:
    (a) Theodosius II
    (b) Emperor Justinian
    (c) Empress Theodora
    (d) General Belisarius
Using encyclopedias and
other reference books,
find out some details of
their lives.

The Eastern Empire Holds On

Although the Roman Empire in the west of Europe collapsed, the Eastern Empire at Constantinople held on for much longer. Unlike Rome, Constantinople had two very able emperors in the fifth and sixth centuries. One of these was Theodosius II.

Theodosius built three walls and a moat to protect Constantinople. The walls were nine meters (about 30 feet) high and stretched across the peninsula of Constantinople. The walls were not broken down by attackers until 1453—a remarkable achievement. Theodosius II was successful in blunting the attacks of the barbarians from across the Danube River. He did this by bribing them not to attack and at other times by attacking the Goths.

In 527, the emperor Justinian took over the Eastern Empire. With his brilliant wife, Theodora, he ruled until 565. Justinian had a clever general named Belisarius. He not only defended the Eastern Empire but won back territory for the emperor. Belisarius led an army to North Africa in 533 and defeated the Vandals.

Emperor Justinian issued a set of laws called the Body of Civil Law. In this book he wrote down all the Roman laws of the past. This code of laws was applied to his empire. Later, kings from western Europe copied his laws, especially those for inheriting land and for the treatment of criminals.

This Eastern Empire was so strong that it did not finally fall until the Turks captured Constantinople in 1453. Certainly the Roman Empire of the East helped to keep eastern Europe in good order until about 700.

Trouble Again

By 700 it looked like Europe was at last calming down. The barbarians had settled down on their small farms. A new system of village life had replaced the old Roman towns. Although the old Roman Empire had gone, the people were united under the Christian church. Monasteries were becoming centers of learning where the knowledge of the past was being preserved and copied. Constantinople was still the safe capital of the Eastern Empire.

In the 700s two new waves of invaders swept across Europe. First came the Muslim Arab invasion. In the 600s, Arab armies had captured Persia, Syria, Israel, northern India, and Egypt. Arab armies swept across North Africa to Morocco, capturing the cities and peoples of this rich area. In 711 the Arab armies crossed the Strait of Gibraltar into southern Europe. The Arab Muslims captured Spain and southern France. Finally in 732 their armies were turned back at the Battle of Tours in France. The Arab Muslims were pushed back into Spain where they settled for the next 500 years.

The Muslim invasion of North Africa and Spain was violent and bloody. The Christians had a long prayer called the "Litany of the Saints," which included a list of things that they wished to be saved from. Some of the Christian churches later added a new part to the prayer because they were terrified of the Muslim invaders: "From the fury of Infidel, Good Lord deliver us." (The Muslims also referred to the Christians as the "Infidels.")

The Arab Muslim invasion and settlement of the Mediterranean region brought new learning to Europe. The Arabs were pioneers in algebra and geometry. Their methods in medicine were far superior to the knowledge of the West. Their building methods added a new chapter to the history of architecture.

Northern Europeans knew little about this Muslim invasion. They were busy establishing Saxon kingdoms in England and Germany. Then from 780 onward a new terror came from the sea: the Norsemen or Vikings. At first they came as raiders, like the Saxons. Then they began to settle in England, Iceland, and Greenland. The Vikings were mainly from Norway and Denmark. Another group of Vikings, the Swedes, migrated up the rivers into central Russia. Like the rest of the invaders, these Vikings settled down to live in their new countries. Their major contributions to Europe were their knowledge of the sea and their exploration of the Atlantic Ocean.

The rest of this chapter will focus on the Arabs and the Vikings.

Activity
Consult an encyclopedia
or other reference books
to learn how Islam spread
throughout Arabia and
the Middle East, and also
how the Muslim Arabs
moved into Europe, Asia,
and northern Africa. Draw
a map or series of maps
showing where the Mus-
lims were during the Mid-
dle Ages.

The Arab Muslims

The Arabs who invaded and settled the Mediterranean were **Muslims**, or followers of the religion of **Islam**. The founder of Islam was the prophet Muhammad, who was born in the Arab city of Mecca in AD 570.

Muhammad

The prophet Muhammad belonged to an Arab tribe. At the time that he was born, the Arab peoples worshiped many different gods. Muhammad taught that there was only one God, Allah, and that he was God's messenger. He taught that people must submit to God. The word *Islam* means *submission* in Arabic. A Muslim is "one who submits" to God.

At first Muhammad was persecuted for his teachings, but later he was accepted as a prophet. In 632 Muhammad died, but the Arab tribes were united under a new religion with Mecca as its spiritual center.

The Koran

The **Koran** is the holy book of the Muslims. It records the revelations that came to Muhammad. It teaches Muslims how they must live in order to submit themselves to God's will.

The most important message of the Koran is that "There is no other God but Allah, and Muhammad is God's prophet."

The Koran also teaches the "Four Pillars" of Islam. These are the four acts of faith that all Muslims must perform.

1. Prayer five times a day

2. Almsgiving (giving money to the poor and needy)

3. Fasting during **Ramadan**, the ninth month in the Muslim calendar

4. Pilgrimage, or **hajj**, to Mecca at least once in one's lifetime

In addition to the Four Pillars of Islam, the Koran includes many other teachings about how Muslims should live. Muslims are forbidden to gamble, drink alcohol, or eat pork. They are also forbidden to practice idolatry (worshiping an object as a god). This rule is so strict that Muslims do not include pictures of people or animals in their artwork. Like the Bible, the Koran also forbids lying, stealing, adultery, and murder.

Write and Discuss
1. Who was the founder of Islam? How did Islam spread?

2. What are the Four Pillars of Islam? What are some of the other beliefs of Islam?

The Koran includes many rules for how people should live together in families and communities. The Koran teaches that husbands are allowed up to four wives—but only if they can treat each wife with equal kindness and fairness. Women are taught that they should be obedient to their husbands and that they should keep themselves covered in public. However, women are also given rights to protect themselves from their husbands.

The rewards for living in submission to God are great. The Koran says that after they die, "soldiers of Allah" will live in a garden of paradise. The garden is full of comforts and peace. Unbelievers instead will be thrown into a hell filled with burning winds and black smoke.

Muslims as Preservers

Most European Christians during the Middle Ages thought of the Muslim Arabs as destroyers. But the Muslims preserved as much as they destroyed. The Muslim Arabs and Syrians lived in the Middle East—the link between Asia and Europe. All around them, kingdoms rose and fell. The Hindu kingdoms of India, Persia, and Greece all faded away, and it was the Muslims who picked up the broken pieces.

As the Arabs moved westward into Europe, they carried learning with them. The chart shows only a part of what they knew and taught to the people of Europe.

Origin of Knowledge	Knowledge Carried to Europe from Arabia or Syria
India and Arabia	Arabic number writing system: 0, 1, 2, 3, 4, 5, 6, 7, 8, 9
Greece and Arabia	Geometry and algebra, especially the idea of algebraic equations
Arabia	The idea of longitude and latitude on maps to give positions in the world
Greece and Islamic Persia	The Persian doctor Avicenna (980–1037) wrote the *Canon of Medicine* in Arabic. Over 40 separate editions of this medical encyclopedia were printed in Latin throughout Europe in the fifteenth and sixteenth centuries, 500 years after his death.
China	The Arabs introduced silk making and paper making from the trade routes to China.

186

■ *An Islamic mosque, or place of worship.*

Write and Discuss
What were some of the Arab contributions in mathematics, architecture, and medicine? Look in an encyclopedia or other reference book to see if you can learn more about Arab knowledge in any of these areas.

Islamic Architecture

Islamic architecture was another important contribution. Islamic buildings had specific purposes. Domes covered shrines, tombs, and sometimes wells. Towers were built for callers to summon the people to prayer. Many buildings were open squares with colonnades of internal archways around the square. Arab and North African travelers could camp in the square and find shelter from the sun in the arched verandahs. These open-square buildings gave the nomadic travelers shelter from the wind and the sun as well as from robbers who roamed the deserts.

The Vikings

The lack of written records means that it is hard for us to know why the Vikings left their homes to raid and settle beyond the seas. Historians suggest several reasons why the Vikings left their homelands in Scandinavia (in what is now Denmark, Norway, and Sweden):

1. The Vikings never liked the idea of a single king. By AD 950, kings were uniting Norway and Denmark. Small groups of unhappy Vikings sailed off for free lands where they did not have to obey anyone. In Iceland they resisted having a single king.

2. The Vikings had the tools to explore and settle faraway lands. They developed a ship that could sail the stormy North Sea. The ship had a **keel**, a long piece of wood along the bottom.

Write and Discuss

1. What factors encouraged the Vikings to leave Norway, Denmark, and Sweden and spread across the North Sea and south into Russia?

2. What improvements did the Vikings make in ships and navigation that helped them make such long voyages as far as North America?

The keel kept the ship from rolling and made it easier to steer.

The Vikings also developed a simple magnetic compass. With the compass and their knowledge of the stars, they were able to leave the shores and sail directly to England—and beyond. Even on a stormy, dark night, they could sail through the rain and clouds with their simple north-south compass hanging from a spar at the stern of the ship.

3. Like many emigrants, the Vikings left their home because of overpopulation. There was not enough land to go around. Like the Saxons, they found good soil on the east coast of England. What started as annual visits became permanent settlement.

4. As Norway and Denmark became Christian, some older Vikings rebelled against the new Christian controls. They sailed off to follow their old pagan ways of raiding and killing. England, Normandy, and Iceland were lands to start anew, away from customs that no longer suited the wilder spirits.

5. Human greed was the motive. By 700, the Saxons were mainly Christians. The monasteries became treasure houses where silver and gold plate were used in church ceremonies. The churches became wealthy with gifts of gold and silver from the people. Usually these monasteries and churches were safe from Saxons, who respected their own religion. But this was not so for the Vikings. Some of these monasteries, such as Lindisfarne, were remote places on islands or on rivers. In 793, the monastery of Lindisfarne was destroyed. The pagan Vikings saw the monks as easy targets, and soon no church or monastery on the east coast of England was safe from the Vikings.

■ *The Viking settlements.*

1   700–800   Faroes, Shetlands, Orkneys, Hebrides
2   820–900   Russian settlements
3   840–870   Ireland
4   870–930   Iceland
5   876–900   Danelaw
6   911–940   Normandy
7   980–1000 Greenland
8   1060–1090 Sicily
9   1100   Crusading Kingdoms

The Vikings Raid Wessex

Written records about the Vikings are scarce. One important record of the Vikings in England is the Saxon Chronicles. The Saxon Chronicles tell the story of how the Danes, a Viking tribe, first raided Wessex in 789.

> This was the year that King Brihtric married Eadbur, the daughter of King Offa. This was also the year that the first Danes reached the shores of Wessex. The king's representative at Dorchester heard of their landing. He thought they were foreign merchants, not enemies. With several soldiers, Beaduherd, the king's official, rode to the coast to order them to present themselves at the king's court. The Danes did not parley with the king's party but killed them outright. This was the first time that the Vikings came to the English shores.

■ *A Viking raider of the English coast—eighth century.*

Activities

1. This is a picture of a Viking before he left home on a raid. Use an encyclopedia or other reference book to learn about some of the objects in this picture. What can you find out about Viking longhouses and longboats, or about the fjords (inland waterways between steep cliffs)?

2. The battle helmet of the Vikings did not have horns on it like you see in some pictures. In a battle, how would the helmet in this picture be an advantage over a helmet with horns?

3. What three weapons does this Viking carry? In what situations would he use each of these weapons?

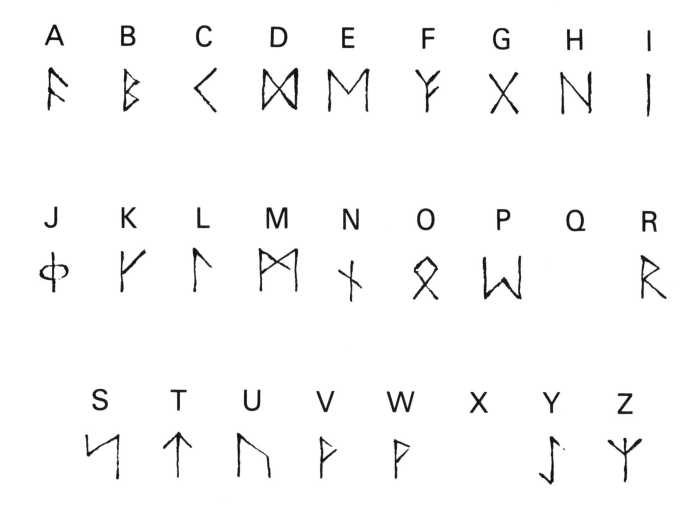

■ *Runic alphabet.*

Activities

1. Write a secret message using the Viking runic alphabet.

2. Use an encyclopedia or other reference book to research the Kensington rune stone. Where was the Kensington rune stone found? What does it appear to be? Do you think the Kensington rune stone is real or a forgery? Why?

The Runic Alphabet

Although there are few written historical records of the Vikings, this does not mean that the Vikings did not write anything. The Vikings carved messages on stone and wood. Many of the messages had to do with magic and spells. They were carved before the Viking people were converted to Christianity. Some of the messages had to do with battles or heroes or landmarks.

The Vikings used a runic alphabet. Because the alphabet was used for carving stone or wood, none of the **runes** has curved lines. The table shows a basic runic alphabet.

Archaeologists have discovered thousands of Viking carvings with runes. Most of the carvings date from the 800s to the 1000s. After the Vikings were converted to Christianity, the Latin alphabet (which is used today for most modern European languages) gradually replaced the runic alphabet.

Time Line of the Middle Ages

AD 381—Gothic King Athanaric visits Constantinople

400—Visigoths migrate across Danube into Roman Empire

406—Vandals cross Rhine River into Germany

410—Roman troops leave Britain to defend mainland Europe; Alaric, leader of the Goths, captures Rome

420—Vandals move through Spain into North Africa

425—Vortigern, king of Kent, invites Jutes to help him fight the Picts

451—Attila and Huns cross the Rhine River into Gaul

455—Vandals from North Africa attack and destroy Rome

476—Last Roman emperor replaced by German king

488—Ostrogoth King Theodoric rules Italy until 526

500—Saxons land in force and set up kingdoms in England

530—Eastern Emperor Justinian stabilizes Eastern Empire by strong rule until 565

570—Muhammad born in Arab city of Mecca

597—Augustine lands in Kent to bring Christianity to Saxons

632—Muhammad dies; spread of Islam

711—Arab armies occupy Spain and southern France

732—Islamic army stopped at Battle of Tours in France

789—Vikings land at Wessex near Dorset, England

793—Vikings attack Lindisfarne Monastery, Northumberland

839—Vikings begin to raid monasteries in Ireland

860—Danes begin to settle in eastern England (East Anglia and Mercia)

870—Settlement of Iceland by Vikings

878—Saxon King Alfred defeats Danes and reestablishes Saxon control of eastern England

886—King Alfred makes a treaty of friendship with Danes in east England

Activity

Here is a crossword puzzle for you to solve. In it are names of people, places, and things related to the Middle Ages.

Across

3. Ruler of Eastern Empire 527–565.
4. Invaded Britain in 410 from the north.
7. "Non-Roman" invaders.
9. Norse raider.
11. Crossed the Rhine River in 406 and later sacked Rome.
12. Pilgrimage to Mecca.
14. Hadrian's _____.
15. Special kind of church.
17. The United States now, or Europe in the Middle Ages.
19. Invaders from the east.
23. Found in 1950 in a bog in Denmark.
25. City in Italy.
27. Form of math brought by Muslim Arabs from Arabia.
29. Viking improvement in ships.
30. The Arabs were important _____, carrying goods and knowledge between the East and West.

32. Legendary king of Britain.
33. Having to do with the Middle Ages.

Down
1. Saxon houses were made of wattle and _____.
2. English place name that came from the Saxon language.
5. Capital of the Eastern Empire.
6. Period of time from about 500–1500.
8. Early English is known as _____-Saxon.
10. Religion founded by Muhammad.
13. The Tollund Man was a _____.
16. Leader of the Huns.
18. A lord in medieval Europe.
20. Holy book of Islam.
21. Viking alphabet letter.
22. Prayer is the first _____ of Islam.
24. Part of the defense built around Constantinople.
26. Means "one who submits" to God.
28. Tribe that considered the Romans superhuman.
31. What monks did from 11 a.m. to noon.

Epilogue
The End of the Story

The human story as yet has no end. This book has looked at just a few parts of history. It began with the Stone Age. Stone Age people left no written records, but archaeologists have been able to reconstruct how the early hunters and growers lived.

Civilization on a large scale started in the river valleys of China, India, Mesopotamia, and Egypt. This book concentrated on Egypt, the land of the pharoahs and pyramids.

We looked at Israel as a key country that had a strong influence on later developments in Europe and the world, especially in law and in ways of thinking and believing.

Greece and Rome were two key areas of European civilization. Western concepts of democracy, art, law, architecture, government, and language came from these two countries.

While Greece and Rome were developing, a separate civilization was developing in the river valleys of China. This Chinese civilization was largely isolated from the Europeans until recent times.

However, the Huns of northern China affected both China and Europe. The Huns helped to unite China under its first emperor. A little later the same Huns began to move westward against the tribes of central Europe. This spilled a huge migration over the borders of the Roman Empire in the fifth century. What followed was a confused period of settling down after centuries of Roman order and control.

The next stage of the story is that small, feudal kingdoms combined into the large, unified kingdoms of France, Spain, Austria, Russia, and England. This time is roughly termed the *Middle Ages,* which ended in about 1500.

This book has not told in detail the human stories of Asia, America, Africa, and India. Now that you know something about the Ancient World, you can learn even more about other countries and cultures on your own. There are many exciting stories still to read, and many histories to explore. Enjoy!

Glossary

anthropology The study of human beings. **Anthropologists** study how people live and relate to one another. They also study how groups of people are similar to or different from one another.

archaeology The study of fossil remains, buildings, and other records of the past. **Archaeologists** study ruins and remains to learn how ancient peoples lived.

argon potassium dating A method for measuring the amount of radioactivity in bones and other remains to determine how old they are.

Buddhism A religion based on the teachings of Siddhartha Gautama (about 563–483 BC). Buddhism teaches that suffering is a part of life. People can be released from suffering if they live moral lives and if they meditate on spiritual matters.

caravel A fifteenth- and sixteenth-century sailing ship with three masts. Caravels were capable of traveling long distances, even against the wind.

carbon dating A method for measuring the amount of carbon 14 in bones and other remains to determine how old they are. A more modern method of dating bones and remains is *argon potassium dating.*

carnivorous Meat-eating.

character A written symbol that stands for a word, especially in the Chinese language.

Christianity A religion based on the teachings of Jesus Christ (0–AD 33). Christianity is based on the Bible and teaches that there is one God. Jesus, God's son, died and was resurrected to save people from their sins.

churl A peasant in the Middle Ages. Churls were freemen (not slaves, like the *serfs*) and often owned some land.

communism A form of government in which a single political party controls all business and other parts of the society. In theory, all property belongs to the people in the society.

Confucianism A philosophy based on the teachings of Confucius (about 551–479 BC). Confucianism teaches that people must behave honestly toward one another and obey the rules of society. Confucianism is sometimes called a religion, but it does not teach about God or gods. Instead, it is a way of life.

consul One of the chief magistrates in the Roman republic.

Corinthian The most elaborate of the three styles of Greek architecture. Corinthian columns have capitals (tops) with elaborate leaves carved on them.

crop rotation A method of farming by which fields are regularly planted with different crops and also allowed to lie fallow (remain unplanted) on a regular basis. This gives the soil a chance to rest and restores nutrients.

democracy A form of government in which the majority rules. Usually democracies have some kind of election to choose leaders to represent the people.

demotic A simplified form of Egyptian *hieroglyphic writing*. Demotic writing is wedge-shaped and easy to carve.

Doric The simplest of the three styles of Greek architecture. Doric columns have capitals (tops) that are plain and square.

dynasty A line of rulers all descended from the same family.

Evolution Theory The idea that the world came into existence over a period of many thousands of years. Evolution is a process of gradual change.

feudalism A system of government in which a lord, or *thane,* rules and owns the land. Peasants swear loyalty to and fight and work for the lord. In return, the lord protects the peasants and gives them a place to live.

fossil The remains of a plant or animal that have been preserved and have become hardened like rock.

geology The study of the earth. **Geologists** study rocks and soil to learn about the earth's history.

hajj A pilgrimage to the city of Mecca, in Saudi Arabia. All followers of *Islam* are expected to make this pilgrimage at least once in their lives.

hastatus (*pl.* **hastati**) In the old, republican Roman army, a foot soldier in the first line.

herbivorous Plant-eating.

hieratic A slightly simplified form of Egyptian *hieroglyphic writing*. Hieratic writing looks somewhat like modern cursive writing.

hieroglyphic writing The picture writing of the Ancient Egyptians.

Homo sapiens Humankind (literally, "wise or intelligent man").

hypothesis An assumption or idea put forward to explain an event. A hypothesis needs to be tested before it can be upgraded to a theory or even to a law.

ideograph A *character* or symbol that represents an idea.

immigration Moving from one place or country and settling in another. **Immigrants** usually move because they are seeking a better life.

Ionic One of the three styles of Greek architecture. Ionic columns have capitals (tops) that have scroll- or spiral-shaped sides.

Islam A religion based on the teachings of Muhammad (about AD 570–632). Islam is based on the *Koran* and teaches that there is one God (Allah) and that Muhammad is God's prophet. *Islam* means *submission*; those who submit are called *Muslims*.

Judaism A religion based on the Bible. Judaism teaches that there is one God and that people must live according to the teachings of the Bible.

ka In Ancient Egypt, the soul or spirit of a person.

keel A long piece of wood along the bottom of a boat. The keel helps prevent the boat from rolling over and makes it easier to steer.

Koran The holy book of the religion of *Islam*. The Koran contains the teachings of the prophet Muhammad.

legionary In the imperial Roman army, a professional solider.

mastaba An ancient Egyptian tomb.

medieval Having to do with the *Middle Ages*.

Middle Ages The period of time from about 500–1500 AD in Europe.

monastery A church, first founded in the Middle Ages, that provided housing for monks. The monks lived, worked, and prayed in the monastery. (Women who lived monastic lives were called *nuns* and lived in convents.)

Muslim A follower of the religion of *Islam*. *Muslim* means "one who submits" to God's will.

Neolithic A period during the Stone Age from about 8000–3000 BC. During this period, people used polished and finshed stone tools.

nome A province, or small state, in Ancient Egypt. **Nomarchs** ruled the provinces.

Nuclear Age The period of time from 1945 (when the first atomic bomb exploded) until today.

oligarchy A form of government in which a small group of people rules.

omnivorous Both plant- and meat-eating.

ostracon A clay tablet with writing on it. In Ancient Athens, an ostracon was used to vote on who was the most unpopular man in Athens. Anyone who received more than 6,000 votes was banished.

Paleolithic A period during the Stone Age that covers all human history before 8000 BC.

patrician A member of the wealthy citizen class of Ancient Rome.

pediment In Greek architecture, the triangular space above the columns and below the roof of a building.

perspective A way of drawing so that things look natural and in proportion to one another. Things that are far away are drawn smaller; things that are near are drawn larger.

philosophy Beliefs and attitudes about life. **Philosophers** seek wisdom and understanding and try to explain their ideas about life.

phonetic language A language based on sounds (phonemes). Phonetic languages have alphabets. Each alphabet letter represents one of the sounds in the language.

phonogram A symbol or character that represents a word, a syllable, or a sound (phoneme).

pictograph A character or symbol that represents an idea.

plebeian A common person in the Roman republic.

praetorian guard The guard of the Roman emperors.

principe In the old, republican Roman army, a foot soldier in the second line.

Ramadan The ninth month in the *Muslim* calendar. All followers of *Islam* are expected to mark the month with fasting from dawn to dusk. (Muslims who are ill or pregnant are excused from the fasts.)

republic   a form of government in which elected leaders and officials govern.

rune   A symbol or character in the alphabet used by the Vikings and other northern European people.

serf   A slave or servant in the *Middle Ages*. Serfs worked their lord's, or *thane*'s, land and could not own land of their own.

shadoof   A system of transferring water for irrigation. A shadoof is a balance with a weight on one end and a kind of bucket on the other.

slash-and-burn   A system of clearing land of trees and other plants before planting crops. Trees and plants are cut down and burned, and the ashes fertilize the soil. After a year or two of planting, slash-and-burn farmers leave a field to grow over, and they cut and burn a new area to plant.

thane   A lord and landholder in the *Middle Ages*. Under *feudalism*, the thane owned the land, and the peasants (*serfs*) swore loyalty and fought and worked for the thane.

tone language   A language based on pitch or tone of voice. The meaning of a word depends on the pitch used in saying the word.

triarius (*pl.* **triarii**)   In the old, republican Roman army, a foot soldier in the third line.

tribune   In the Roman republic, one of the senators elected to represent the *plebeians*, or common people.

trireme   An Ancient Greek fighting ship with three rows of rowers. The many rowers meant that triremes were very fast.

veles (*pl.* **velites**)   In the old, republican Roman army, a frontrunner. The velites were lightly armed and attacked the enemy first, before the main Roman army attacked.

Zealots   In the first century AD, a group of Jews who fought against the Roman occupation of Israel.

ziggurat   A pyramid-shaped tower with spiral steps around the outside.

Index

Page numbers in italics indicate illustrations

A
Aborigines, 15
Achilles, 80–81, 82
Aegean Islands, *81*
Afterlife, Egyptian belief in, 35, 42
Agriculture
  in China, 137, 158–60, *159*
  in Egypt, 25, 27, 28, *28*, 55
  in Middle Ages, 178, *178, 179*
  slash-and-burn system, 20, *21*
Agrippina, 111
Akhenaton, 32, *32*
Alanis, 170
Alaric, 169
Alexander the Great, 67, 98, 101
  expeditions of, *98*, 99–100
Alexandria, 59
Alfred, King of Wessex, 175
Alphabet
  Chinese, 140, 161, *162–63*
  development of, 78, *79*
  Greek, *79*
  Phoenician, *79*
  runic, 189, *189*
Amenemhet III, 30

Amon, 30
Angles, 172
Animal fossils, 6, *7*
Animal hunts, 130
Anthropologists, 10, 16
Anubis, 42
Archaeologists, 15–16
Architecture
  Egyptian, *32*, 33, *34, 40*, 41, *41*, 50–51, *50*
  Greek, 102–4, *102, 103*
  Islamic, 186, *186*
  Roman, 111–12, *112, 113*, 125–28, *125, 126, 128*
Argon potassium dating, 10
Ark of Covenant, 62, 65, 66
Army
  Chinese, 164
  Egyptian, 50
  Roman, 116–24, *117, 119, 120, 123*
Art
  Chinese, 146, *146*
  Egyptian, 33, 52–54
  Greek, 103–4, *104, 105*
Arthur, King, 175
Assyria, 58
Assyrians, 67

Aswan Dam, 27, 55
Atbara River, 25
Athanaric, King, 168
Athens, 88–89, 96
Attila the Hun, 170, 171
Augustine, 174
Ausonius, 133
Australia, 15

B
Babylon, 17, 18, *18*, 67
Beijing, 155
Belisarius, 182
Benedict of Nursia, 180
Bible
  New Testament, 73
  Old Testament, 54
Bi Sheng, 145, *145*
Blue Nile River, 25
Body of Civil Law, 182
Bones, determining age of, 10
Britain
  ancient, 174–75, *174, 175*, 177–78, *177*
  Christianity, 174–75
  language, 176
  in Middle Ages, 172–73
  Roman rule, 112
Bronze Age, 4
Buddhism, 157

C
Caesar Vespasian Augustus, 123
Cairo, 25, 55
Canaanites, 62
Cannae, Battle of, 118
Cantonese, 161
Caravel, 156
Carbon dating, 10
Carthage, 59, 101
Cassandra, 82
Catullus, 135
Censor, 109
Central America, 16
Centurions, 121, *121*
Champollion, Jean François, 45
Character. *See* Alphabet
Chariots, 31, *31*
China, 16, 24, 58
  agriculture, 137, 158–60, *159*
  Buddhism, 157
  Communist People's Republic, 164
  Confucianism, 157
  Cultural Revolution, 164
  development of writing, 161–63, *162, 163*
  Empress Wu, 147–49, *148*
  European invaders, 155–58
  Han dynasty, 143

Hun invasion, 149–50, *151*
inventions and improvements, 143–46
language, 161, 163
Ming dynasty, 151–52
Qing dynasty, 155
rivers, 137, *137, 138*
Shang dynasty, 138
Shi Hwangdi, 139–40, *139*
size and variety, 136–37
Yuan dynasty, 151
Zhou dynasty, 138
Chios, 93, 94
Christianity, 58
  beginning of, 69–70
  in Britain, 174–75
  and legacy of ancient Israel, 72–73
  in Middle Ages, 179–81, *180, 181*
  in Roman Empire, 114–15
Churls, 178
Circus Maximus, 129
Cleisthenes, 89
Colosseum, 111, 112
Confucianism, 157
Constantine, 114–15
Constantinople, 59, 105, 115, 168, 182, *182*
Consuls, 107, 108
Copper Age, 4
Corinth, 97
Corinthian columns, 102, *102*
Crassus, 109
Creation theories, 3
Crete, 103
Crop rotation, 160, *160*, 178, *179*
Crusades, 73–74
Cultural Revolution, in China, 164
Cyrus of Persia, 67

D
Darius, 93
Dark Ages, 4
David, King, 68
  capture of Jerusalem, 64–65
  death of, 66
Dead Sea Scrolls, 60
Democracy, 88–89
Didius Julianus, 113–14
Djoser, 40
Doric columns, 102, *102*

E
Ecclesia, 89
Egypt, 17, 29
  agriculture, 25, 27, 28, *28*, 55
  architecture, *32, 33, 34, 40*, 41, *41*, 50–51, *50*
  art, 33, 52–54
  Assyrian invasion, 33
  burial process in, 35–40, *37, 38, 39, 40*

capital of, 25, 28, 29, 55
control of Suez Canal, 55
early dynasties, 29
First Intermediate Period, 30
foreign invaders, 55
government, 30
Late Kingdom, 34–35
life of common people, 48–49
life of soldiers, 50
Middle Kingdom, 30
New Kingdom, 32
Nile Valley, 25–27, 28
Old Kingdom, 29
pharaohs, 28–29, 33
population, 55
relations with Israel, 55, 75
religion, 30, 32, 35, 42
and river civilizations, 24–25
seasons, 25, 27
Second Intermediate Period, 31
Third Intermediate Period, 33
tombs and pyramids, 40–41
in twentieth century, 54–55
writings, 43–46, 46
Ekron, 64
Electrical Machine Age, 4
Embalming bodies, 36, 38
Empire Age, 4
Eskimos, 15
Ethiopia, 25
Euboea, 94
Euphrates River, 61
Evans, Sir Arthur, 84, 103
Evolution, 3, 6

F
Far East, 58
Feudalism, 138
Flavius Josephus, 70
Fossils, 6, 7, 11
France, 183
Franks, 171, 177

G
Gaius Marius, 120
Galba, 111
Gath, 64
Gaul, 171, 177
Genghis Khan, 150–151
George III (England), 157
Gihon Spring, 65
Giza, 29, 41
Gladiators, 129, 130
Gordium, 99
Goths, 105, 168
Great Pyramid of Giza, 29, 41
Great Sphinx, 29, 41

Great Wall of China, 141
building, 140, 152–53, 153
cross section view of, 152
defense measures, 154
end of, 155
gates in, 150, 154
reasons for building, 149–50, 169
second, 150–52
Greece, 58, 81
alphabet, 78, 79
architecture, 102–4, 102, 103
art in, 103–4, 104, 105
Athens, 88–89, 96
downfall of, 101
importance of, 78
independence from Turkey, 105
invasion of Israel, 67
legends, 79–84
literature, 79–84
Mycenaean, 83–84, 84
Olympic Games, 90–93
Persian invasion, 93–95, 96
Roman rule, 105
Sparta, 85–88, 86, 87, 95, 96
time line, 85
Greek Orthodox Church, 105
Guangzhou (Canton), 161

H
Hadrian, 112–13
Hadrian's Wall, 174
Hajj, 184
Han dynasty, 143
Hannibal, 101, 118, 119
Hastati, 116, 118
Hatshepsut, Queen, 32
Hebrew people, 54
in Egypt, 32, 61
settlement in Israel, 61, 62
Hector, 80, 81
Helen, 80, 82
Hellespont, 95
Helots, 86
Herod, King, 69
Herodotus, 35
Hieratic writing, 45
Hieroglyphic writing, 43
History, ages of, 3–4
Hittites, 62
Homer, 79, 83
Homo erectus, 9, 9
Homo habilis, 9, 9
Homo sapiens, 8
dating existence of, 11–12
early, 9, 9
modern, 9, 9
skull of, 11

Horus, 42
Houses
  Egyptian, 50–51
  Roman, 125–28, *125, 126, 128*
Huang He River, 137, 138, 152
Human life
  ages of, 2
  development of, 8, 9, *9*
  estimating age of, 10
Huns
  invasion of China, 149–50, *151*
  invasion of Greece, 105
  invasion of Rome, *115,* 169, *169,* 170
Hyksos kings, 31
Hypotheses, 24

I
Ice Age(s), 11, *12, 13*
Ideographs, 162
Iliad, 79–81, 83
Illuminated manuscripts, 181
Immigrants, 166–67
India, 16, 24, 100
Ionic columns, 102, *102*
Iran, 75
Iraq, 75
Iron Age, 4
Isaiah, 67
Isis, 42
Islam, 58. See also Muslims
  architecture, 186, *186*
  beliefs of, 184–85, *185*
Israel, 55. *See also* Jerusalem
  building of temple, 66, *66*
  captivity of, 68–69
  capture of Jerusalem, 64–65
  end of ancient, 67, 70–71, *71*
  geography, 58
  Hebrew settlement in, 62
  Jewish State of, 74–75, *75*
  legacy, 72–73
  relations with Arab countries, 55, 75
  religious importance, 58
  Roman occupation, 69
  twelve tribes, 62, *63*
  twilight years, 73–74
  written history, 59–61
Israelites, 62, 64

J
Jacob, 62
Japan, 58
Jerusalem, 59, 64–65
  destruction of, 67
  Muslim control, 73–74
  old city, *76*
  temple, 66, *66*

Jesus Christ, 69–70
Jewish people, 59–61
Jordan, 75
Judaism, 54, 58
Julius Caesar, 109
Justinian, 182
Jutes, 172–73, 174
Juvenal, 133–34

K
Ka, 40
Kamose, 31
Keel, 186–87
Khufu, 41
Knossos, 84, 103
Koran, 184–85
Kublai Khan, 151, 155

L
Lake Trasimene, Battle of, 118
Language. *See also* Alphabet
  Chinese, 161, 163
  English, 176
Lebanon, 66, 75
Legate, 120
Legionary, 120, 121, 122, *123*
Leonidas, King, 95
Lesbos, 93, 94
Libya, 75
Licinius, 114
Lindisfarne, 187
Li Ssu, 141
Literature
  Greek, 79–84
  Muslim, 184–85
  Roman, 129, 132, 133–35

M
Macedonia, 95
  under Alexander the Great, 98–101, *98*
  rise of, 96–97
Manchu invaders, 155
Mandarin Chinese, 161
Mao Zedong, 163, 164
Marathon, 93, 94
Marco Polo, 155
Marcus Aurelius, 135
Masada, 70–71, 111
Mastaba, 40, *40*
Material civilization, growth of, 17–18
Maxentius, 114
Medieval Europe. *See* Middle Ages
Memphis, Egypt, 28, 29, 30
Menelaus, 80
Menes, King, 28–29, *29*
Meng, General, 140
Mentuhotep II, 30

Micah, 69
Middle Ages, 4
   barbarian invasions, 167–71, *168, 169, 170*
   in Britain, 172–173
   Crusades, 73–74
   life in, 179
   monasteries, 180–81, *180, 181*
   Muslim invasion, 183
   time line, 190
   Vikings, 183
Middle East, 58
Miletus, 93, 94
Ming dynasty, 151–52
Minoan civilization, 84, *84*
Monasteries, 180–81, *180, 181*
Mongols, 150
Monte Cassino, 180
Moses, 61
Motor Age, 4
Mount Li, 141–42
Muhammad, 184
Mummius, 101
Muslims
   architecture, 186, *186*
   beliefs, 184–85, *185*
   control of Jerusalem, 73–74
   invasions, 105, 183
Mycenae, 83–84

N
Naxos, 94
Neanderthals, 9, *9*
Nearchus, 101
Nebuchadnezzar, 67
Necho II, 34
Neolithic Age, 16
Neolithic people, 15–16, *17,* 19–22, *19, 20, 21, 23*
Nero, 92, 133, 134–35
New Guinea, 19–22, *19, 20, 21, 23*
New Stone Age, 16
New Stone Age people, 15–16, *17,* 19–22, *19, 20, 21, 23*
New Testament, 73
Nile Valley. *See* Egypt
Nineveh, 67
Nomarchs, 30
Nomes, 30
North Africa, 183
Nubia, 29
Nuclear Age, 2, 4

O
Octavia, 111
Octavius, 109
Odyssey, 79

Old Stone Age, 15, *15*
Old Stone Age people, 14, 16
Old Testament, 59
Oligarchy, 89
Olympic games, 90–91
   ancient, 91–93, *92*
Osiris, 42
Ostracon, 89, *90*

P
Paleolithic people, 14, 15, *15,* 16
Palestine, 75
Palestinian Arabs, 74
Paper, 144–45
Paris, 80
Parthenon, *89*
Patricians, 107
Pericles, 88
Persia, 58, 93–95, *96*
Pertinax, 113
Pharaohs, 28–29
   burial of, 35–40, *37–40*
   foreign, 33
Pheidippides, 93
Philip V (Macedonia), 97, *97,* 101
Philistines, 62, 64
Philosophy, Roman, 133–35
Phoenicia, 65, 66
Phoenician alphabet, 79
Phonetic language, 161
Phonograms, 45
Piankhi, 33
Pictographs, 162
Picts, 174
Plant fossils, 6, *7*
Plebeians, 107
Pompeii, 127
Pompey, 109
Pontifex, 109
Pottery
   Chinese, 146, *146*
   Greek, 104, *104, 105*
Praetorian guard, 113
Praetors, 108
Prefect, 121
Priam, King, 83
Principes, 116
Printing, 145–46
Pro-consuls, 108
Psamtik III, 34
Ptolemy, 101
Ptolemy V, 45
Public baths, 131, *131*
Pyramids, 29, 40–41
   construction of, *41*
   mysteries of, 41
   writings inside, 48–49

Q

Qin Dynasty, 161
Qing dynasty, 155
Quaestor, 109

R

Ramadan, 184
Re, 42, *42*
Religion. *See also* Buddhism; Christianity; Islam
  in Egypt, 29, 30, 32, 35, 42
  paleolithic, 14
  theories on beginning of life, 3
Remus, 106
Republic, 106–7
Ricci, Matteo, 156–57, *156*
River civilizations, 24–25
Rome, 4, 59, 109–10, *110*
  army, 116–24, *117, 119, 120, 123*
  barbarian invasions, 115, *115*, 135
  under Constantine, 114–15
  Eastern Empire, 115, 182
  entertainment, 129–31, *130, 131*
  under Hadrian, 112–13
  under Julianus, 113–14
  kings, 106
  literature, 129, 132, 133–35
  and Masada rebellion, 70–71, *72*
  under Nero, 111, *111*
  philosophers, 133–35
  republic of, 106–9, *107, 108*
  rule of Greece, 101, 105
  rule of Israel, 67
  under Vespasian, 111–12
Romulus, 106
Rosetta Stone, 45, *46*
Runes, 189, *189*

S

Sadat, Anwar, 55
Saladin, 74
Salamis, 95
Samaritans, 67
Samians, 94
Samos, 93
Sarcophagus, 41
Saul, 64
Saxon Chronicles, 188
Saxons, 172, *172*, 177, 187
Schliemann, Heinrich, 83, *83*
Schliemann, Sophia, 83
Scots, 174
Senate, Roman, 107, *107, 108*
Seneca, 129, 132, 133
Sennacherib, King, 67, *68*
Septimius Severus, 114
Shadoof, 27
Shang dynasty, 138

Sheshonk, 33
Shi Huangdi, 139–41, *139*
Shiloh, 62
Shi Yuangdi, 141–43, *142*
Sidon, 65
Silk, 143–44, *144*
Silk route, 155
Silva, 70
Slash-and-burn system, 20, *21*
Solomon, King, 67, 68
Spain
  Muslim invasion, 183
  Sueves, 170
  Vandals, 170
  Visigoths, 169
Sparta, 85–86, 96
  life in, 86–87, *86, 87*
  Persian invasion, 95, *96*
Step pyramid, 40, *40*
Stone Age, 4
  beginning of human life on earth, 8
  Homo sapiens, 11–12
  end of, 18
  establishing dates in, 10
  Neolithic people, 15–16, 19–22, *19, 20, 21, 23*
  Paleolithic people, 14
Sueves, 170
Suez Canal, 55
Sumer, 17, 61
Swedes, 183
Syracuse, 91
Syria, 75

T

Tacitus, 134–35
Tang Gaozong, 147–49
Tang Taizong, 147
Tarquinius Superbus, 106
Ten Commandments, 62
Terence, 133
Thailand, 16
Thane, 177
Thebes, 30, 95, 96
Theodora, 182
Theodoric, 170, 171
Theodosius II, 170, 182
Thermopylae, 95, *96*
Thessaly, 95
Thoth, 42
Thutmose III, 32
Tiananmen Square, 164
Titus, 70, 111
Tollund Man, 172, 173, *173*
Tombs, 40–41. *See also* Pyramids
  Egyptian, 33, 40, 51
  Chinese, 141–43, *142*
Tone language, 161

Tours, Battle of, 183
Trajan, 130
Triarii, 116
Tribunes, 107, 108, 121
Trireme, 93–94, *94*
Trojan horse, 82, *82*
Troy, legend of, 79–83
Turkey, 105
Tutankhamen, 32
   tomb of, 32, *32*, 51
Tyrant, 89
Tyre, fall of, 99, *99*

U
Urban Age, 4

V
Vandals, 105, 170, 182
Velites, 116
Vespasian, 111–12
Vikings, 183, 186–88, *187, 188*
Visigoths, 169
Vortigern, 174

W
Wessex, Viking raid of, 188
White Nile River, 25
World War II, 105
Wu, Empress, 147–49, *148*

X
Xerxes, 94–95
Xu Da, 152

Y
Yangtze River, 137, 138
Yellow River, 137, 138, 152
Yuan dynasty, 151

Z
Zealots, 70–71, *71*
Zhou dynasty, 138
Zhou Enlai, 164
Ziggurat, *34*
Zionism, 74
Zuh Yuanzhang, 152